STARTUP
TO
SOLD

HOW I BUILT MY SIDE HUSTLE INTO A
MULTIMILLION-DOLLAR BUSINESS

CHUCK TEMPLE

AN INC.
ORIGINAL

This publication is designed to provide accurate and authoritative information in regard to the subject matter covered. It is sold with the understanding that the publisher and author are not engaged in rendering legal, accounting, or other professional services. Nothing herein shall create an attorney-client relationship, and nothing herein shall constitute legal advice or a solicitation to offer legal advice. If legal advice or other expert assistance is required, the services of a competent professional should be sought.

An Inc. Original
New York, New York
www.anincoriginal.com

Distributed by River Grove Books

Design and composition by Greenleaf Book Group
Cover design by Greenleaf Book Group and Hannah Gaskamp and Will Tams / The Collective Spark Creative

Publisher's Cataloging-in-Publication data is available.

Print ISBN: 978-1-63909-014-3

eBook ISBN: 978-1-63909-015-0

First Edition

CONTENTS

PART II: TO SOLD

AN ENTREPRENEUR OF OPPORTUNITY

I didn't spend my youth dreaming of becoming an entrepreneur. On the contrary, I stumbled my way onto that path. I was what some call an "entrepreneur of opportunity"—discovering a market need that wasn't being filled well by existing providers, and jumping in with both feet to fill the gap. Over the course of six years, I started and, with a lot of help, developed what became a very successful business called DVD Your Memories. When I stepped away, I sold it for more money than I'd ever dreamed of having.

I was a psychology major in college, not a business student. So I wasn't exactly well prepared to jump into entrepreneurship. But I did it anyway. That meant embarking on an endless journey to educate myself in all things related to starting up and growing a business. It meant learning some lessons the hard way.

What you'll find in *Startup to Sold* is the story of my first entrepreneurial venture—and adventure—from my days as a nearly broke college student to my last day with DVD Your Memories, which at that time (just seven years after I started it) had twenty-seven full-time employees and millions of dollars in annual revenue.

If you are, as I was, someone without a business background who wants to launch a sustainable business, I hope you'll learn from my mistakes and successes and pick up some tips on how to survive this kind of challenging but rewarding path. If you have a business background, I hope my story will inspire you and remind you how to be successful.

Either way, I hope you'll enjoy the ride!

AUTHOR'S NOTE

Along with the information contained in this book, I've also created a reference website at startuptosold.com containing up-to-date resources. At the end of most chapters, you'll find a section titled "Online Resources" listing articles and blog posts available on startuptosold.com that provide further information on each chapter's topic areas.

PART I

STARTUP

CHAPTER 1

LEARNING HOW TO SUCCEED AT ANYTHING

Becoming an entrepreneur involves a steep learning curve. If you're an expert in a certain field, you have to learn about running a business. If you're a business major, you have to learn about the market niche you want to fill. When I launched the business that became DVD Your Memories, I fell into the first category. But luckily, even before that point, I had the general mentality that I wanted to succeed at whatever I was doing, and that meant *learning* how to succeed.

The lessons that would serve me well later in life started coming hard and fast during my sophomore year in college. Back then, I was always a few hundred dollars away from being broke.

LEARNING TO REFINE A SALES PITCH

If you have ever been broke—I mean really broke, where you can't afford to go out and eat with your friends or take someone out on a date—you know the kind of broke I'm speaking of. During my sophomore year of college, my bank account balance fell below $100, and I had to move home for nine months to make enough money so I could get back to school. I drove my rusted 1982 Honda Civic wagon from San Diego State University back to my hometown of Davis, California, a suburb of Sacramento. I found my first sales job, standing in front of stores and asking people to sign petitions. If they did, I would get between $0.75 and $1.50 per signature.

I'm not a born salesman, and I was never known for having any kind of natural charisma or charm. But when you are forced to make someone like you within a split second, over and over, you can develop the skill of being likable. I had to approach about a thousand people per day. They would be walking up to the store and see me. Within a second, I could see they were silently judging me. And that is how long I had to make an impression.

Now, I can't tell you the secret to making someone like you within one second, but I can tell you that it has something to do with affection and positivity. If I could show myself as affable and nonthreatening, that would go quite a long way.

Of course, some people would just pretend they didn't see me, or they would offer a negative reply they had drummed up while I began to approach them. But the coolest part of this job was noticing the progress. I could see day after day, after thousands of trials, my percentage of signatures going higher and higher, and people stopped ignoring.

I learned two valuable lessons during this time. The first was that under the right circumstances, my own efforts were in direct proportion to the amount of money I earned. If I screwed around and took a million breaks, I wouldn't have very many signatures, and I wouldn't make much money. But if I worked my ass off and hustled, I could make about $15 to $20 per hour, which at the time was the most money I had ever made.

Most jobs available to young people are hourly based, so it doesn't matter how well you work or how efficient you are, because you will still collect a paycheck. In this way, our brains are trained to do the least possible "work" in the most amount of time. This mindset maximizes your overall advantage. But learning this type of system is what makes average employees, not entrepreneurs. In the brain of an entrepreneur, there is a direct, unavoidable link between the action taken and the reward.

The second lesson was how to fine-tune a sales pitch—not only the initial pitch, but my response to customers depending on what they said. In time, I learned how to be prepared for any scenario. For example, if someone told me that they didn't have time to read the petition, I had a perfect answer—an answer that I had tested over thousands of trials and knew was the most effective.

For example, my typical opening would be, "Do you have thirty seconds to sign the school bus safety initiative?" To which the person would reply, "I actually don't have time to read through it right now." When I first started out, I would let the person simply walk away. But after some trial and error, I realized people usually thought that by signing, they were making a deciding vote. Why else would they say they needed time to read the paraphernalia?

So I began to respond by reassuring them, "Signing doesn't mean you're voting for it. It just allows the issue to get on the ballot. You can decide later how you want to vote, when you have more time."

With more rejection came more fine-tuning, until eventually I had two and even three people signing my petitions—at the same time! Within a couple months, even with no sales training or background, I broke all records for my employer.

Then I found another company whose petitions were much more valuable—one for $1.25, another for $1.75, and one for $2.25 per signature! If I got someone to sign all three, that would be more than $5 in one shot. Once I switched companies, I averaged $60 an hour. Don't get me wrong: the money was great. But the work was exhausting. Having a thousand conversations a week and being "on" all the time drains your mental and physical energy even more than you would expect.

Once the political season ended, I wanted to try my hand at another type of sales job, so I picked the most quintessential sales job there is: selling used cars. This job turned out to be valuable for reasons I wouldn't understand until I owned my own business; at one dealership in Davis, I learned how I *didn't* want to operate.

That's not to say the job was all bad. Even with other people trying to steal your "ups," there was a lot of camaraderie. I remember it as mostly a fun time, full of watching the Sacramento Kings' epic playoffs against the Los Angeles Lakers. (I still can't believe they called Mike Bibby for that foul against Kobe Bryant.) But mostly I learned *what not to do* when running a business.

For instance, a PhD student from University of California at Davis called to inquire about a car. Since she didn't own a car, the owner of the dealership told me to pick her up from campus and bring her to the dealership. I was given one more instruction: "Make sure she buys a car before she leaves." I didn't realize how serious the owner was about this last point.

I showed the woman at least ten cars. Unfortunately, none were to her liking. After a few more rounds of my boss saying, "Chuck, go show her another car out there," I started to feel bad about essentially holding this person hostage.

Another hour of this dance was about all I could take. I finally caved and took the woman back to the university so she could resume her day. I got a serious warning about getting fired because I took the customer back to campus without making a sale. I didn't argue, but I noted something important: I am not comfortable treating customers as only a means to an end.

Another day, some customers came in to look at the "loss leader"—a car that was advertised specifically to get people in the door, but if it were sold, the company would take a loss. Of course, everyone wanted to check out the below-cost vehicle. So while I was instructed to show the customers every car besides the one that lured them in, they found their own way to the loss-leader vehicle and started opening doors and taking a closer look.

The owner noticed this and came over to make small talk with the customers, trying to persuade them to look at other vehicles. But they wouldn't budge. Finally, pointing to the loss-leader car, he said, "Is this the car you want?"

"Yes," they responded without hesitation.

"You don't want this car. This car is not for you!" the owner exclaimed as he proceeded to kick the driver's side door in with his boot.

Needless to say, these experiences made customers (and me) feel uncomfortable. How a business treats its customers becomes that company's reputation, and a bad reputation eventually kills a business. Years later, I learned that this dealership didn't survive—and I had a hunch as to why.

Tip: Dictate Your Own Future

There are two types of people in this world. The first type allows outside circumstances to dictate where their life will lead; they let life control them. The second type learns that they can change their own life—that they can dictate where the future leads and create their own opportunities. It is the second type of person who can become a successful entrepreneur.

During the nine months I spent working petitions and selling cars, I learned to take some control over my own life and

continued

discovered that I could influence outcomes. I'd watched so many movies growing up that I thought everything in life would just turn out okay no matter what I did, like a good ending to a movie. But that type of thinking was not logical, and all it got me was the difficulty and stress of being broke and having to leave school. Plainly speaking, I learned that where a laissez-faire attitude could work for some people—those who had a big safety net or a cushion to fall back on—it wouldn't work in my situation. I had to rely on myself to learn what I needed to learn and then put that knowledge to good use. It was that attitude that led me to the path of becoming an entrepreneur.

LEARNING TO MOTIVATE WITH NUMBERS

With $10,000 in hand earned from the work I did back at home, I re-enrolled in San Diego State. But I still had to work and make money. And thanks to my recent experience in sales, I got a job selling digital cameras at a big-box electronics store in the Mission Valley area of San Diego. During the previous year of working petitions, I had started to see myself as someone who could perfect a sales pitch, and I took this same mentality to my new job.

It was around 2003, and digital cameras were getting hot with consumers. I started working at the Mission Valley store a few weeks before Thanksgiving, and I was heavily trained just in time for Black Friday. Our instructions were to "upsell" by persuading customers to buy the recommended service plans and accessories. The service plans were just like a warranty, and useful for digital cameras because they are so fragile. The accessories I was instructed to sell included a memory card, a camera case, and an extra battery. I challenged myself to become one of the top salespeople at the store.

The general manager was aware of my sales background and made a deal with me upon getting hired. "If you sell well over the holiday season," he told me, "I will see to it you receive a good raise early next year." With that incentive, I worked my ass off.

My new buddy and coworker, Yiga, and I set off to become great camera salesmen. Yiga started at the store around the same time as I did. We strategized together about the different pitches we would use and what we would say depending on objections the customer raised. Over time we became successful camera salesmen and even better friends.

Somehow management had convinced the employees to sell as if we were on commission, without actually giving any sort of commission. Employees were even offended if customers turned down their upsell offers. Coming from jobs where I was paid mainly on commission, I was dumbfounded and curious to learn how the company accomplished this psychological feat.

After a few months I realized management's strategy, and it was nothing short of brilliant. Every hour or two, the sales managers would share reports with the various departments. There was a lot of energy surrounding those reports because they showed each department its "numbers": our percentage of upsells and our ranking within the local area and even the company at large. We could track how we were doing for that day and for the month. This constant updating of information engaged our team because it gave us nearly real-time metrics on our performance.

Salespeople would be happy if the numbers looked good and unhappy if the numbers looked bad. Other electronics stores paid their employees on commission, while this one saved money by showing its employees some numbers every few hours.

Brilliant!

Lesson Learned:
Broken Promises Destroy Motivation

After Black Friday and the subsequent holiday season, I asked the general manager of the store about the raise he had promised me. I reminded him how well our department was doing and how I had contributed to the performance.

"Raises are frozen," he replied. "Sorry, Chuck. Nothing I can do."

And just like that, what I had learned from petition selling—that my effort could directly affect my result—was completely contradicted. From then on, I clocked in at 3:07 for my shift that started at 3:00, because I learned how the time clocks rounded up or down. I started doing the least I could while still getting my paycheck, because I had lost trust in the company.

LEARNING TO TRUST MYSELF

I sold electronics thirty hours a week for three years while pursuing a psychology degree full time at San Diego State. Eventually I left my job in electronics to become a behavioral tutor for children with autism. Working with these children was an extremely challenging job, and especially so given that it was my first time working with children. My job as tutor went hand in hand with the information I was learning in my psychology classes—in particular, one called Learning and Behavior, which introduced me to the teachings of Paul Chance and operant conditioning. Operant conditioning, in a nutshell, is how we reinforce behavior (sometimes good and sometimes bad) and get the best out of everyone.

I was still in training when I started working with six-year-old

Timothy at his home outside of San Diego. Cute as can be, Timothy was a whirlwind, or more like a tornado—running around the house, playing with everything, and leaving messes everywhere. His overwhelmed parents told me school was useless, as Timothy would not listen to his teachers and generally ran amok. But the worst part was, he would regularly run out of the house and get lost in the neighborhood.

My trainer accompanied me to Timothy's house for the first week. Timothy would not listen to us. I could see he was having a good time while we tried every trick in the book to get him to focus or work on a puzzle or just sit down in his little plastic chair for ten seconds. Instead of doing what we asked, Timothy would run around the room, climb on furniture, tiptoe along the windowsill, and jump on his bed. After that week, when my trainer's duty was done, her parting words to me were something akin to "Good luck."

Completely on my own the following Monday, I did the only thing I had left to do: nothing.

I literally gave Timothy no attention. I knew that giving reinforcement after bad behavior would lead to the increased frequency of the behavior. And I had learned that some children don't care what kind of form reinforcement comes in—positive or negative, reinforcement is still a response. Often parents don't realize they are reinforcing their children's bad behaviors by giving them attention, whether good or bad. Sometimes children who are ignored would rather have negative attention than no attention at all. Actually, this applies to anyone, not just children.

My first day alone with Timothy started as it had the previous week, with Timothy refusing to listen and do his work. I was in his room with my left hand on the door so he couldn't escape and I could keep my eyes on him. My feet were spread wide, and I looked straight ahead, avoiding eye contact with Timothy at all costs. After getting tired of climbing the walls of his room, he moved on to throwing blocks into the air and sometimes at me. I'll admit, I did flinch a few times, but otherwise I stood motionless, even when hit with a block.

Toward the end of my two-hour session, Timothy turned up the volume on his bad behavior. He grabbed my arm—the one posted against the door—and began swinging on it as if he were on the monkey bars, kicking over whatever was close to him. Even then I remained statuesque, so he switched tactics and rubbed the skin on my arms until it burned. I didn't so much as look at him. I was bruised, but not beaten. And Timothy showed no signs of letting up, even as the session came to an end.

Our standoff continued on Wednesday during our ninety-minute session. Timothy continued to run through his tactics, graduating to teasing me by saying, "Okay, ready to work now!" This got me to look over to him, but as soon as I did, he would jump up faster than a jackrabbit and start laughing at me. I tried every-thing, offering him small toys and candy when he was really ready to start his work. Wednesday came and went with no progress.

I drove over to Timothy's house once again on Friday for my last session of the week. The first hour went by the same way as before. But finally, with one hour left, something changed. Timothy sat down in his plastic chair at the small Fisher-Price desk and reluc-tantly said, "Okay, I'm ready to work now." These were the same words he'd spoken before, but this time there was a hint of final-ity to them.

With all the nonchalance I was capable of, I said, "Okay," and casually walked over to the table. I rewarded Timothy with an M&M and proceeded to open a children's book to read. Timothy didn't jump up after he got his treat, but continued to sit patiently, looking at me expectantly as if I were a friend he had missed and was happy to see. I wondered if he could understand that the subdued smile on my face was hiding a fierce, powerful inner feeling of pride in what we had just accomplished.

From that day forward, Timothy listened to me and trusted my resolve. He no longer jumped around the room but waited for me in his chair. We had a lot of fun over the next couple months, working together at home and taking walks around his neighborhood without him running off and getting lost. His progress affected his school experience, according to his beaming mother, who told me Timothy was finally listening to her and his teachers.

Shortly thereafter, Timothy's family moved away, so I don't know what happened with Timothy as he grew up. I hope he knows that through working with him, I learned a great deal about grit, patience, and—well, learning.

I also learned about trusting yourself: if you believe you are on the right track, run with it, and don't let anyone (especially yourself) tell you otherwise.

THE LESSONS COME HOME TO ROOST

Learning how to *refine* a sales pitch . . . learning how *motivating* numbers could be . . . learning to *trust* what I knew—I didn't appreciate the significance of these lessons at the time, but all of them proved useful when I launched my business.

I knew that it was unlikely I would have a perfect sales pitch right out of the gate, so I was prepared to test and refine, and then test and refine again. I appreciated that numbers are important, so I wasn't afraid to find the right mix that would provide the right motivations for me as I shaped the business. And I had learned to trust my instincts and be resolute—perhaps the most important lesson in my first year in business, when I spent four months straight with my hand on the proverbial door, working twelve-plus-hour days while losing money. The experience with Timothy taught me that when you think all is lost and you're hanging by a thread, the most miraculous things can happen.

Had I told you up front that three keys to my business success would be found in stories about getting people to sign a petition, selling used cars, and working with a six-year-old on the autism spectrum, would you have believed me? Probably not. And I'm not saying that you need to have those same experiences. But if you've worked hard and succeeded at *anything*, I'm willing to bet there is a lesson in there somewhere. Think about those successes, and remember them during the challenging or hard times you face.

You never know when those unlikely lessons might come in handy.

Online Resources: Foundations of an Entrepreneur

Visit startuptosold.com for up-to-date resources on the following topics.

- Best jobs for establishing good work ethic

- How to refine a sales pitch

- Operant conditioning basics

CHAPTER 2

SOMETIMES YOU NEED CHUTZPAH

A s you can probably tell already, I didn't start out with a grand plan to become a technology entrepreneur. And while I wouldn't change my experiences with gathering signatures, selling cars, or working with Timothy, none of these beckoned to me as a potential career. Fortunately, my somewhat convoluted journey brought me onto a path that eventually did lead to a business opportunity that perfectly suited my talents and abilities. All I had to do was have confidence in the skills I already had—and enough chutzpah to take me into areas I didn't know so well.

Here's how that happened.

STEP-BY-STEP DOWN THE TECH PATH

I tutored children for another year and a half while continuing to pursue my degree, until around 2005, when a completely different opportunity came along. Yiga, my fellow camera salesman and good friend at the electronics store, remembered I had computer skills and an obsession for all things technology. So when his mom's computer was on the fritz, he asked if I could help.

Maybe it is time for a change, I thought. I had spent the previous five years in college making just over minimum wage. And because I wasn't making much money, I had to work a lot of hours just to survive. But I hadn't fixed computers since high school, when I helped out in my mom's office. I was hesitant but desperate—and even more important, I was open to serendipitous opportunities like Yiga's.

Ultimately, I agreed to look at his mom's computer. I was a little rusty, but I managed to solve her problem. And being a nerd again didn't feel so bad!

Not long after I fixed her computer, Yiga's mom referred me to someone else—a co-owner of Market Grocer, a local grocery store. He had some computers in the main office that were misbehaving and needed someone to fix them. Still nervous that my skills were rusty and I wouldn't be able to fix their problems, I decided that if this gig worked out, I would stop trying to turn off the techie side of myself. I love computers, I felt good about fixing them, and the pay was pretty decent. In a way, my decision to work with Market Grocer felt like I was coming home.

I met Islam, the general manager of Market Grocer, which was not just a small corner store. It had about ten registers, twelve aisles, and twenty or thirty employees. I only needed about two days to fix all the old machines at the market. They were good as new, and I was a hero for a few minutes.

A few weeks later Islam gave me a new task, something I had not done before. Because he thought of me as the "computer guy," he presumed I was an expert with all technology. Islam asked if I could create the market's weekly print ad. It just so happened that I had a digital camera from the electronics store and a copy of Photoshop software, so I was good to go!

I didn't have to create the ad from scratch, as there was a template already built. I just changed it according to the specs I was given: new price, new dates, and sometimes new products on sale that I would take pictures of with my digital camera and then cut and paste into the ad. It was a pretty easy job, and I got paid my requested $15 an hour to do it.

After a few months of good work, Islam asked me about building a website. Now this was something I had to pause and think about. Making a small, one-page website for a freelancer was one thing, but creating a website for a grocery store with lots of cyber traffic and ever-changing information was totally different. And I had only dabbled in web design, making exactly one terrible-looking personal web page. I was neither a coder nor a designer, and the Market Grocer site would need twenty or thirty pages.

The question was, did I have the skills to do it?

PUSHING MY OWN BOUNDARIES

As I said above, sometimes you need to have chutzpah, even if at times it can get you in trouble. I had no business trying to learn HTML and CSS (cascading style sheets) while I was already busy with tutoring and going to school. But I was foolish and excited to learn, so I bit off a little more than I could chew, putting myself in the position of having to really scramble to acquire new skills.

I went back to the apartment I shared with four roommates (plus one or two friends who would crash on our couch sometimes), and began educating myself on the art of website building. I spent the next few months in my bedroom testing different software programs. Each had its limitations, and I would spend a day or two building something only to scrap it later. Weeks went by with very little progress. I don't even want to think about how many hours I spent struggling with this project.

I hope you won't think less of me—and that the statute of limitations has expired when I tell you how I ended up with a twenty-page website for Market Grocer. But since I only made $2,000 for the entire project, I'll take the risk. Because there was no way I could have developed this website on my own—and from scratch—I started looking at the sites of other grocery stores, especially ones farther away and under the radar on the East Coast. This kind of research was useful; it helped inspire me and illustrated to me the elements of sites that were well done. Certain fonts, contrast in colors, and how heavy to take the copy were some of the things I observed and stored away for future use.

Based on everything I saw and learned, I ended up backward-engineering what eventually became the new website for Market Grocer. And it was a big deal. Everyone loved the way it looked, and the new color scheme matched the company well. I also came up with a couple of marketing strategies for the website, like a weekly text message notification system of sale items, which may have been relatively novel to the industry at the time.

But that wasn't the coolest part. There was a recipe section on the website, and whatever recipe was featured showed up in a little box on every other page. Since the site was new, and no one had submitted recipes with pictures, I decided to post my recipe for sun-dried tomato hummus. My recipe appeared on every page of the website. Only a few folks ever noticed that recipe in the little side box, but something else did notice it—the Yahoo search engine, which was the search engine of choice back in the day.

I had no idea, but the fact that the recipe was linked on every page gave that recipe a lot of link-juice. The analytics program showed a ton of traffic coming in from the keywords "sun-dried tomato hummus." I typed those words into Yahoo, and lo and behold, my recipe was the number two result in the world! Market Grocer was getting visitors from all around the globe to view my sun-dried tomato hummus recipe. It was an accidental discovery that made an unexpected difference for my client while also providing a nice introduction into search engine optimization—something that would become very important in my future career as a business owner.

HOW TO MANIPULATE A NERD

I continued to create the weekly ad for Market Grocer while working as a behavioral tutor for children with autism. During my final year of college, Islam introduced me to Daniel, a retiree, world traveler, and movie aficionado.

As it turned out, Daniel always attended an annual film festival at a friend's house. This was not a small film festival, but a five-night affair for fellow globetrotting aficionados who wanted to present slideshows of their trips. There was a popcorn machine, a projector screen, and even a microphone for presenters. Each night, one or two people would present their slideshows.

One of these amateur filmmakers had recently used software to make a DVD of the slideshow rather than the usual slide projector or PowerPoint method. Daniel was intrigued, as this not only was a simpler method of presentation, but allowed for more features such as timed background music. Daniel wanted to figure out how he could get his PowerPoints onto DVD to play at his film festival.

"Chuck," he said, "I'm not sure this can be done, because none of the other computer guys have been able to figure it out. I think it shouldn't be too hard, but maybe it is. I've got all my images in order on the file including transitions. But I want them to play with these CDs that I purchased from each country. Right now, I must play the CD in a separate CD player and then attach my laptop to a projector. It would be so much easier just to play the DVD. Do you think this can be done?"

I was in before he even got to the second sentence. Whatever it was, I would figure it out—or die trying. I mean, my reputation as a computer guy was at stake.

That night I went home and made a test PowerPoint presentation, and found some DVD authoring software. I couldn't figure out how to get it to work, so I called my dad. He is the one who gave me the computer nerd genes, so it made sense to go to the source.

We spoke on the subject for a while and tested some stuff out. Then my dad suggested some screen recording software called Camtasia. First we ripped the CD to an audio file on the computer, and then we played both the PowerPoint and the audio simultaneously, so Camtasia would record the PowerPoint and music at the same time. Then we would take that video file and burn it to a DVD. Simple!

Tip: Play to an Expert's Vanity

Fun fact about computer people and, I suspect, any other kind of expert: they take a lot of pride in their skills. And if you ask them a question *in the right way*, they will go to the ends of the earth to figure it out. Here's how you ask them: "No one has been able to figure this out, so it may not be possible, but . . ." and then you ask them the question. I'm not sure if Daniel knew this secret method, but he used it on me nonetheless. And it worked like a charm.

I came back to Daniel a couple days later with the good news. He hired me to work with him to convert about eighty of his PowerPoint decks to DVDs with music. We worked from his house nearly every day. We would set up both his laptop and my own and complete two to four productions every evening. The two of us watched each finalized DVD, with Daniel narrating the story of each trip, accompanied by a related drink from his vast collection of liquors from around the world.

Looking back at these years, I had gone from barely surviving on minimum wage to getting paid two or three times that much to sit back and drink fancy liquors. Something had changed in me when I was broke and left college—and I decided to do whatever I had to in order to not be broke anymore.

That intention directed me on a path where one person, one opportunity, led to the next—Yiga introduced me to his mom, who introduced me to Islam, who introduced me to Daniel. And eventually Daniel would introduce me to someone who would give me the greatest challenge.

THE WORLD BECOMES MY PLAYGROUND

Things were finally starting to get better. My whole life I had been broke or nearly broke, and for the first time I had a little extra money in the bank. It was my turn to take an exotic trip. This trip would change the direction of my life, but I didn't know that at the time—the story just unfolded that way, as it always does in life.

I had been to Mexico, Israel, and Canada, but nothing as "exotic" to me as Thailand, so I used my extra earnings to head off on a spring break adventure with three of my friends, including my pal Gabe. The trip was full of ups and downs: great food, humidity, purchasing formal suits while being served beer, getting sick, boat rides, and a few stitches in my head. Oh, and some skinny dipping. It was wonderful.

Following in Daniel's footsteps, I manifested my images from that trip into a DVD slideshow, complete with titles, videos, images, songs, and some crazy interviews. The four of us from the trip went with Daniel to the film festival that year and presented the Thailand DVD to our middle-aged and senior audience members. It was a sort of tour de force, showing off what could be done with the latest consumer-grade DVD editing and authoring software. But most of all, it was fun using all those computer skills to put together something so creative and self-indulgent.

Following that spring break trip, I finally graduated from college in June 2006, six years after I entered the doors of San Diego State. My buddy Yiga and I brewed some of the tastiest beer ever for my huge graduation party. I played the Thailand slideshow for both sides of my family. My roommate Mike bartended all night. At the very end of the night—when most of my family had left and just a few friends remained, scattered around our house—I stumbled outside. As I looked up at the clear, expansive sky, I had a revelation.

When we are young, our parents tell us everything: where to go, what to eat, what we can and cannot do. Then as we get older, in junior high and high school, we get a little more freedom, maybe choosing what classes to take or sports to play. Some people feel like they can do whatever they want after high school, but I felt like I needed to go to college. Even though I got to choose my direction more than ever before, I still felt like I was not fully in control. It was as though I started off in a narrow tunnel, which got wider and wider as I got older, the light of freedom getting brighter and brighter.

As I looked up into the sky that night, I realized I was finally out of that tunnel. At that moment, I felt I could do anything I wanted in this world.

I decided to see how far I could go in this new world that had just opened. I wanted to see what I was capable of when I had only myself to listen to. I wanted to see how far I could go before hitting a wall. The world was my new playground, and I was inspired to test its limits.

Online Resources: Quick-Start Business Resources

Visit startuptosold.com for up-to-date resources on the following topics.

- Favorite website builders

- My used-to-be world-famous sun-dried tomato hummus recipe

- Best software for making slideshow videos on PC and on Mac

- How to build a text message notification system in 5 minutes

CHAPTER 3

A BUSINESS IS BORN

My original plan for after college was to go back to Thailand and teach English for six to twelve months. Then I would apply to the Computational Neurobiology doctorate program at the University of California San Diego. I had completed all the prerequisites and had close to a 4.0 GPA in my psychology classes, so I figured I could probably get in.

I remember checking Dave's ESL Café (an online job board for English teachers) every day, looking at the different jobs in all the cities in Thailand, fantasizing about the adventures I might have. In preparation for my great escape, at the end of the school year my roommates and I had a big garage sale. I sold my desktop computer, all my furniture, and even my surfboard. I would have sold my old textbooks as well, but some lady walked off with them. The only things I had left were my laptop, a few items of clothing, and a car to put them in.

Having all my possessions fit into my car was also helpful because now I was homeless. After graduation, most of my roommates went off to different places, and only two were still in San Diego, living together in an apartment. I alternated between living on their couch near San Diego State and living with another couple of friends, Ben and Steve, over in Pacific Beach.

I never realized what a bother I must have been, assuming I could crash in my friends' living rooms whenever I wanted. When you are struggling, you have a hard time seeing something from another perspective. I was always struggling, so I never thought much about what it was like to have a guy taking up space in your apartment all the time.

As it happened, that best-laid plan to teach in Thailand never came to fruition. Real life intervened, in the form of Victor.

ESTABLISHING A FOOTHOLD

Around the same time as graduation, Daniel introduced me to his friend Victor. He had at least two thousand slides that hadn't yet been converted to digital format, and he hired me to help him digitize them. I suggested we use a slide scanner, even though I had never used one before and had to quickly tutor myself in how one works.

First you set up forty to fifty slides on a tray. Each slide needs to be oriented in the right direction and with the proper side facing out, so there is less need later for digital rotation or flipping. Then you start up the scanner and wait one to three minutes per slide scan. Victor's machine was quick and took about one minute per slide, so I had to wait about an hour until I could put in the next batch of slides.

During the wait time, I tried to teach Victor how to use the machine. I edited the scanned slides in Photoshop for levels, white balance, and color correction. Victor, who was paying me by the hour, began to complain about the cost of me sitting in his house for half the time, not working on anything. I explained that with one slide scanner, there was nothing more I could do besides edit images and make DVDs. A few weeks went by like this, but I didn't particularly enjoy having an unhappy client.

How could I solve this problem?

Victor had a lot of slides, and he was right—since I had 50 percent downtime, the method was not the most efficient. The only thing I could think of was to scan his slides on my own time and charge him by the unit. That would be fair for him, and I wouldn't have to deal with him complaining on the phone or having to drive the thirty-five minutes each way to his house. Yes!

And if I bought my own slide scanner, I could scan the slides for other people too, and make money while doing nothing at my own home! It was a perfect plan—except for one thing. I didn't have a home.

I was living in Pacific Beach at Ben and Steve's apartment at the time, and had assisted Ben a few months earlier with the purchase of his desktop computer. I knew it could handle the slide scanner, and I explained my idea to him, also pointing out that I thought I could attract other clients. I worked out the numbers, and it seemed possible to make about $25 an hour setting up the scanner on Ben's computer and letting it run. We could then go surfing for an hour or so, come back, change the slides, and go out again. Ben liked the idea, so we became partners.

I bought the $1,500 slide scanner, a Nikon Super Coolscan 5000 ED, with my credit card. This was a lot of money for us to spend on a whim, as we were two recent graduates heavily in debt with student loans. Ben created a color-coded invoice on Excel and used it for Victor's first order in our brand-new company.

We picked up the boxes of slides from Victor and transported them to our facility (Ben's bedroom). We opened them, cataloged everything, and high-fived each other. And then Victor rang to let us know he had called around and discovered he could get the same work done at Costco—for twenty-five cents less per slide.

Victor wanted us to match the Costco price or else he was going to take his slides back. Ben and I went from overjoyed to feeling like someone just punched us in the gut.

We looked up how Costco performs slide scanning and learned they ship the slides out to another facility. When we explained to Victor that the third party didn't use the same high-end scanner that we'd bought—and didn't include editing and color correction—he said he didn't care. It felt like he wanted to ruin our business before it even started.

We ended up nearly matching Costco's price, which took all our profit out of his order. We ate the hours of time we spent to get the job done, dealing with (and praying over) a constantly jamming machine. This was not a set-it-and-forget-it process or a quick job, as we had naively thought.

But it still paid for the slide scanner.

Lesson Learned: Businesses Are Complicated

Many entrepreneurs start out the same way I did: by focusing on a specialized talent or area of interest that meets a currently unmet market need. Capability meets a market niche. What would be simpler?

As Ben and I learned, however, businesses are much more complicated than we had envisioned. Each one, no matter how large or small, has a myriad of working parts—machines, orders, customers, technology, employees, landlords (or friends who might kick you out)—and within each of these variables, an unlimited number of things can go wrong.

> This was one of my first lessons in the realities of a new business: that as soon as you think you're on Easy Street, something goes awry.

KEEPING THE FAITH

Ben and I got through Victor's order, beaten but not broken, and we kept the faith that the business could work. We set about to make ourselves more legitimate, beginning with giving the business a name: DVD-Photo-Memories.com (yes, with the dashes and dot-com). Ben made a fantastic brochure that we planned to distribute around San Diego. I can't tell you how many versions of that brochure we made, but in the end we were very proud of it. And we had some business cards printed.

Figure 1: Our first business card for DVD-Photo-Memories.com.

Since I was still planning to go Thailand (I hadn't given up on that dream!), we used only Ben's cell phone number on our marketing materials. Even *my* business card had Ben's phone number on it. We had a lot of fun making our paraphernalia—but we had no customers.

When it came to figuring out sales, Ben and I had very different views. Ben thought he could drum up business by going to La Jolla each day and talking to wealthy people at coffee shops. My idea was to build a website—which can be considered crude at best, as it was a simple template that could be modified to fit an ever-expanding list of services—and set up a booth at farmers markets, showing off a slideshow of our products.

Figure 2: Our first website for DVD-Photo-Memories.com.

Three times a week I would haul a canopy tent, two large wooden folding tables, bins full of our marketing materials, and a 27-inch tube television that weighed over a hundred pounds. All this would somehow fit into the back of my car. After four to five hours of standing and talking to people, I would then spend another hour packing everything back up and hoping that someone would call or email.

We soon learned that Ben was more in tune with the demographics than I was—and how important it is to go where the target customers are. The farmers markets were mainly a bust at first. Many people stopped by and picked up brochures, but not many of them became customers. Ben's idea worked a bit better, but even so, we managed to pick up only a few customers over the next month.

Once those customers realized we were located in a crappy apartment near Highway 5 in Pacific Beach, many of them would just drop off their media without coming in. For others who did find their way inside, we decorated the "office" by putting a tablecloth down on Steve's coffee table and clearing any dirty dishes lying around.

In addition to scanning slides and making DVD movies out of them, we started transferring videotapes and old movie film to DVD. These new services came by way of requests from customers. When they asked for something we couldn't yet handle, I told them we could do it—and then we would scramble to figure it out.

Despite our less-than-professional façade, our list of services was growing.

EXPLORING THE FRONTIERS OF INTERNET MARKETING

In 2006, internet marketing was still new, and only a handful of national companies in our niche knew how to effectively use it. Market Grocer had enjoyed that windfall of traffic via the sun-dried tomato hummus recipe, but by then Yahoo had fallen by the wayside and Google was the main player.

So many people need the *services we provide,* I remember thinking, *but if they are not at a particular farmers market or coffee shop, they will never find us.*

Internet marketing changed this concern. More specifically, PPC—pay-per-click technology—changed all that. With PPC, you could pay to show up at the top of the search results, so when someone typed in "slide scanning to digital," we could pop up first on the page. Now our business could gain a number one ranking, despite having a very amateur website, and a few more people contacted us. It was not a ton of people, but Ben and I were living on a shoestring, so a few orders went a long way.

To me, especially as a college graduate with a degree in psychology, the whole business thing became a fun game to play—maybe the greatest game, in fact, because there were so many types of players, rules that kept changing, and puzzles that kept shifting. I had been broke all my adult life, so I felt I had nothing to lose. If I did go bust, I could rely on my computer skills or go work in Thailand.

With the inspiration from the night of my graduation, I decided to push on, putting Thailand on hold and focusing on taking the business higher.

ON MY OWN AGAIN

Partnerships are hard. I was hooked on figuring out this business game and taking it to the next level by finding an office space ASAP. Ben, on the other hand, couldn't commit to growing the business, so we decided to go our separate ways.

We agreed to dissolve his interest in the business, and neither of us looked back. Ben went on to do well as a headhunter and then moved to France to take care of his grandmother and learn information marketing. We continue to be close friends.

Lesson Learned:
Partnerships Don't Always Work Out

Since the dissolution of my first partnership with Ben, and my experience with other partners, I have come to realize that this type of business arrangement needs to be set up very carefully or else things will get difficult. Maybe someone makes a lifestyle adjustment and doesn't have as much time to devote to the company. Or maybe one person feels like selling their shares and getting out for a more lucrative offer. These are all things that need to be figured out before starting a partnership, while emotion is not clouding anyone's judgment.

You need to plan for every contingency, because something unexpected will eventually happen.

By the autumn of 2006, just a few months after starting DVD-Photo-Memories.com, I was out on my own again. And I was about to experience both the joy and the pain that come from figuring out how to make a business work.

Online Resources: Quick and Easy Marketing

Visit startuptosold.com for up-to-date resources on the following topics.

- Easy tools to design business cards

- Why farmers markets are a good idea to test your product and find your customers

- How to set up internet marketing and test business ideas online

- Basics of Google AdWords

CHAPTER 4

PERSEVERANCE: GETTING A BUSINESS OFF THE GROUND

As summer turned to fall in 2006, I was out on my own again and committed to growing my business. I thought I would start by trying to make an actual salary, although I didn't have any idea how much that was going to be. At the time, my vision of a successful future was earning as much as what I thought my parents made—maybe $4,000 or $5,000 a month. I wasn't sure what it would take to get there, but I was going to do everything I could think of to make a real business out of my endeavor.

It was time to get serious.

A REAL OFFICE

No longer crashing on Steve and Ben's futon, I rented a room from a very nice woman named Julie in Clairemont Mesa, just up the street. She didn't require an application, and the rent was month to month—plus, I could see the fireworks from SeaWorld every night. I jumped at the deal and moved the few things I had into my new bedroom.

Around the same time, I started looking for a real office. I knew that to be taken seriously as a business, I couldn't be operating out of Ben's apartment. I quickly found a small office available at the Law Offices of Richard Roy. He was renting out a back hallway plus one cubicle for $600 a month, no lease involved. It was furnished and included a phone line. The space was centrally located with access to three main freeways. With no lease and month-to-month rent, I thought this was the low-risk business move of a lifetime.

Figures 3 and 4: Me in the company's first office.

Richard Roy was a cool guy. I figured he probably had been in my shoes once, because he was helpful in getting everything started for me. Anything he wasn't using, he would let me borrow. There was a break room with a vending machine, and a conference room that I could book when a client was coming in. I was so excited to have my first real office.

The timing, while not achieved on purpose, was prime. It was September—right at the beginning of the holiday season. And as everyone knows, preserving memories on DVD makes for a great holiday gift.

REFINING MY BUSINESS FOCUS

My father once told me, "You can do a few things really well, or you can do many things not very well." As I was starting to build the business, I didn't think I had a choice to do a few things really well, because no single part of my income stream was enough to make a living. I was supplementing my income in many ways besides transferring old media and doing IT work for several companies.

Meanwhile, DVD-Photo-Memories.com was providing a whole range of services. The website promoted videography services, promotional videos, and even search engine marketing services—anything to make a buck. Despite my dad's advice, I was the jack of all trades and master of none.

Luckily, during a spell of voracious reading about all things business related, I came across a book titled *The 22 Immutable Laws of Branding: How to Build a Product or Service into a World-Class Brand* by Al Ries and Laura Ries. I quote that book to this day—in particular, the following line: "The scope of your services is inversely proportional to the strength of your brand." Read that sentence a couple of times, as it is very important.

The brain remembers simple ideas much faster than complex ones. A business that offers too many disparate services will not be known for any of them. Would you choose a plumber who also washes windows and changes the oil in your car, or a plumber who specializes in plumbing? Most people think that if you are dedicated to one thing, you will be better at it. I wholeheartedly agree.

Consequently, I stopped working on all the other side projects and took the extra services off the website. I wanted customers to know that I was *not* a video production company doing media transfer work on the side. Instead, my refined branding message indicated that I had the only local company available to perform media transfers full time.

The question was, would people notice my dedication to one type of service and reward me with their orders?

AIN'T TOO PROUD TO BEG (FOR ADVICE)

I was too proud to ever ask for money from friends or family, but I never shied away from seeking advice. I didn't know anything about business; almost everyone knew more than I did. After the 2006 holiday season, I spent the downtime learning and thinking about what I wanted to see happen in the future. The name DVD-Photo-Memories.com was not going to fly for the long term—especially the dot-com part. It was time for a name change.

I asked some close friends, family members, and even a few customers to meet me at the office for a brainstorming session. Each person created a list of company names, and we narrowed the list to the top ten. Then we sent that list to about twenty other people for a vote, which narrowed the list to two finalists: Memory Lane DVD and DVD Your Memories.

I liked both names because they conveyed the essence of the

service. We could have chosen a name that was catchy yet didn't directly relate to the service the business was offering. Those types of names cost a lot more in advertising, however, because you must teach the customer what the name means. If you go with a name that describes the service, you can save money.

Tip: Lead a Creative Team through the Funnel

Think of a creative team as a funnel. I know it sounds weird, but quantity is the aim here—not quality. You start with as many ideas as possible, with no regard to the quality of each idea. As you progress through the steps, you will narrow down ideas and the quality will emerge.

1. **Brainstorm.** Start out with each person coming up with ideas on their own—not as a team, with another person, or after seeing another person's work. You do not want any influence here. Each person from your creative team should focus on coming up with as many ideas as possible, focusing on quantity over quality. Determine a numerical goal for each person, along with a deadline.

2. **Streamline.** Once everyone submits their quantity-biased ideas, create a master list of good ideas by removing duplicates and other ideas that simply won't work. Thank everyone for their contribution.

3. **Finalize.** Gather the same team (or a different one), and chat about the remaining ideas. Let people bounce ideas around and elevate some. Try to get down to two or three finalists. If it's an in-house meeting, make sure to provide food and drinks. Thank everyone for their time with gift cards or something similar.

continued

4. **Survey.** Throw the final ideas into a survey. You can easily
do this with Google Forms. Try to make sure the people voting in the survey are part of the target market.

5. **Calculate.** If the survey results are close, use this website to gauge market response to your idea: https://www
.perrymarshall.com/splittester/.

I couldn't decide on a winner. After a few days of thinking, I
thought of a way for thousands of people to vote on the two final
options—my first real crowdsource, and it only cost fifty bucks.

Many people don't realize this, but Google AdWords—now
Google Ads—is one of the best and cheapest platforms for market
research. Typical ads comprise four lines: a headline, two lines of
text, and a website address. I wrote two identical ads, swapping out
each of the business name options.

Memory Lane DVD
100 Year Archival DVD's
On Every Order. Call Now!
www.MemoryLaneDVD.com

DVD Your Memories
100 Year Archival DVD's
On Every Order. Call Now!
www.DVDYourMemories.com

I ran the two ads across the United States for two days. They
would show up in the search results when someone typed in a key-
word that related to my services. After two days, and a total cost

of only $50, there was a definitive statistical winner: Memory Lane DVD had a click-through rate of 4.68 percent, while DVD Your Memories had 5.46 percent. That seems like a minor difference, but I had a large enough sample size that the small difference was statistically significant. Finally, something I had learned in psychology class had paid off!

DOH! ACCOUNTING MATTERS!

By the end of 2006, I had worked a lot and figured out even more. But then the holidays ended, and I had my official introduction to seasonality. I hadn't thought it was important to track my finances, so I had no idea how much money I'd made in the past few months. I just figured that if my bank account balance was increasing each month, then I was doing well.

It seems obvious in hindsight that paying attention to income and expenses is critical for a business. But based on my conversations with other entrepreneurs, I think many of them have the same mindset as I did—at the beginning, there are so many other aspects of business to attend to, ones that feel more urgent and exciting, so keeping track of finances becomes one of the last priorities.

But once 2007 rolled around, company revenue took a nosedive. I realized toward the end of January that my bank account was shrinking—the first time since starting the business that I had experienced a net loss.

And since I didn't keep books, I wasn't even sure how deep that dive really was. I knew I wasn't making as much money as in the previous few months, but instead of turning my attention to something that would be stressful (finances), I chose to ignore it. So many entrepreneurs make this same big mistake—the ostrich burying its head in the sand, as I did. Instead of looking square at the problem, I pushed it away, thinking maybe it was temporary. And I nearly went broke, again, because of it.

By the end of February, I started to get scared. I didn't have much in the way of cash reserves to live on, and those reserves were shrinking fast.

My goal was to make $4,000 to $5,000 per month, and I was accomplishing this goal. So what was the problem? Well, my goal did not take into consideration my business expenses, which were about $5,000 per month—nearly the same as my income. This was a problem, and I suddenly realized why accounting is important. I was netting between zero and $700 per month. My room at Julie's house was $600 per month, which gave me almost nothing (or less than nothing!) to live on.

I always made sure to pay my rent, but I resorted to stealing food from my housemates and the front-desk candy bowl at the law office. Julie would always have rice in the rice cooker. I usually didn't take much, and to this day I wonder if she ever realized I was surviving off her scraps. The rest of my meals consisted of frozen vegetables and Top Ramen—whatever was cheaper at the grocery store.

Scavenging was not a good feeling. I was working harder than ever but making less money than the $9 an hour I'd earned at the electronics store back in college. After February ended without any profit, I became more worried.

What if business doesn't pick up?

Am I going to fail at the first thing I've ever done on my own?

I just invested all my time and money into this business, and now I'm going to be fully bankrupt . . . again.

These were terrible feelings for someone who, just a few months prior, had been so high on the prospect of growing a business in a brand-new niche. Luckily, my mom realized my need for legitimate accounting systems and drove down from Davis to set up

QuickBooks. After that, my good friend Gabe came down from Los Angeles to teach me accounting. Learning from Gabe and my mom was critical to understanding the part of business I had never learned.

But even with their help in getting things off the ground, that freedom I was feeling at my graduation party began to feel more like futility.

Tip: Force Yourself to Become Well-Rounded

If you are going to be a business owner, you must be well-rounded. You must know the difference between cash and accrual, and learn how to not mix personal finances with business. You must figure out how to look at your books so you understand patterns and trends.

Some things come easy, and some things don't. For me, accounting was totally foreign, but the answer was not to shy away from it. To learn it, I had to face it head-on.

A PERSONAL CRISIS

All of my local competitors were video production companies doing media transfer on the side. I began to ask myself: Why would my business work on a model of specializing in transfer? I was running this thing into the ground against all the sensible advice I had received from trusted friends and industry experts, which was mainly: *Get a real job!* I felt like I was on a crazy roller coaster ride, but unlike on most roller coasters, I was going down and totally unsure that I would ever go back up.

And one more thing added to the terrible feeling of dread that was compounding: I had decided to go off Paxil, my antianxiety medication, cold turkey.

During my final semester of college, I knew something was wrong when I started getting panic attacks in class just from the thought of raising my hand. I would be constantly second-guessing myself about whether what I had to say in class was important and how the other students would react to it. This type of thinking made me more and more nervous, which led to increasingly rapid cycles of negative thinking. Eventually I would shut down, lower my hand, and try to recover. One day I didn't recover.

I went to student health services, and the practitioner prescribed me Paxil, an antidepressant that also works well for anxiety. It did wonders for me. Social situations no longer made me feel so nervous, and I was free to say whatever I wanted. I kind of liked it. I got the doctor to keep upping my dosage until few things caused me anxiety at all.

Losing money when you don't have any to spare typically causes tremendous anxiety, especially when you are prone to anxiety like me. But it didn't. I figured Paxil was so good at subduing my anxiety that it was to blame for my inability to see the immediacy of my situation. The final straw was being unable to afford health insurance. Without the coverage I had in college, the prescriptions simply became too much to afford out-of-pocket. So I quit Paxil cold turkey. Which proved to be disastrous.

I won't go over all the side effects of quitting a medication that your body and brain have become accustomed to, but the withdrawal made me feel disoriented, lethargic, depressed. Add that to the hopeless *What the hell is this all for?* feeling—a result of working my ass off while slowly going broke—and suffice it to say I was not too motivated. Each day was the same: Eat poorly. Work all day and into the night. Achieve little reward other than becoming more and more broke. Rinse and repeat.

I had reached a point where I wondered whether everyone was right: DVD Your Memories was not a business that was going to work. Yet something kept me going.

DEFYING LOGIC

When all logic points toward quitting and going back to something known, something easier, something safe and responsible, or even heading to Thailand to teach—there must be a compelling reason not to listen. The reason I had for not quitting defied logic or explanation. Even now it is hard to put into words, maybe because my decision to defy logic was something that can't be described or explained—more of a feeling than a conscious choice.

Call it instinct, that gut feeling that compelled me to keep going. It told me that what I was doing was right, and one way or another, everything would eventually work out. My gut told me to not give up, ever. People needed this service!

And then I remembered back to what I had learned from Timothy, the boy I worked with a few years earlier. Sometimes you must stand with your hand on the door, even though you aren't quite sure if you're doing the right thing. And you will have hours of doubt about what seems like a good idea, fear that you are wasting your time—or worse, fear that you are doing the opposite of what is actually necessary.

I think of it as my passion speaking to me, as passion's existence is not predicated by logic. And when passion is present, you can do one of two things: fight it until you deny it, or let it sweep over you and lead you to the unknown. I chose door number two.

Tip: Decide Whether Your Business Is a
Choice or a Compulsion

Someone once asked me how I knew it was the right choice to continue growing my business. I remember at the time thinking that I
didn't *have* a choice. Instead it felt like the business had chosen *me*
and wouldn't loosen its grip.

Every aspect of the business consumed me. I read every book
about business and entrepreneurship I could. Each conversation
I had, no matter how unrelated, sparked a new idea and circled
back to the business. If you do not have the same kind of obsession, at least in the early stages, it will be very difficult to devote the
kind of time and energy it takes to build a business from scratch.

Not long after deciding I was going to sell the last thing I
could—my car—to continue making DVD Your Memories a success, I read a life-changing book titled *Think and Grow Rich* by
Napoleon Hill. I'd heard about the book from a few people, but it
was a psychology professor who gave it the best recommendation.
He told everyone in that three-hundred-seat auditorium to read
this book once in their lives.

The book was written at the turn of the twentieth century,
when Hill interviewed the most successful people of that era
about the number one reason for their success. I remember reading just the first few chapters and getting the premise: thoughts
can create tangible outcomes. When you truly believe you can
achieve something, and you allow that conscious belief to create
a reality in your subconscious mind, your subconscious will work
overtime to make it a reality.

I took my feeling of limitless boundaries from my graduation party and applied it to being successful in my chosen industry. Despite the problems with finances and debilitating anxiety, I envisioned myself not only making as much money as my parents, but making a limitless profit.

My head and my heart stepped into rhythm, and from that moment on, my thoughts were totally different. Even my subconscious thoughts were different. And I realized something interesting: the mind can be either the most limiting factor in a person's success, or a powerful tool to make unexpected things happen.

Online Resources: Fundamental Business Basics

Visit startuptosold.com for up-to-date resources on the following topics.

- My favorite marketing books

- How to learn accounting

- Bonus—the book that changed my life: *Think and Grow Rich* by Napoleon Hill

CHAPTER 5

UNEXPECTED SUCCESS

I n your wildest dreams, what level of success do you envision for your business? How quickly do you envision it happening? In a month? Six months? A year? Five years? Early in 2007, I became convinced that there was limitless growth potential for my business. Turns out I was right, but what I didn't anticipate was how quickly that growth would occur. And I learned firsthand how it feels to try to outrun a speeding train.

A FEW SECONDS TO DIFFERENTIATE

I have found that business owners are either operationally focused or marketing focused. You can tell when owners are operationally focused, because they will deliver the best product and take a lot of pride in how they get the work done, but their presentation to customers will be lacking. Further, the physical walls of the business will usually be the same color as when they moved in, and the packaging of their products will be utilitarian.

Marketing-focused business owners will be quite the opposite. They will have fancy packaging. Their office will have color, and maybe even some pictures on the wall or murals. They will understand the customer's experience. But their end products will be more middle-of-the-road in terms of quality.

My nature is 100 percent operationally focused. I can sell just fine once I find someone with a need, but attracting that someone is a different story. I operate on ones and zeros; either something works or it doesn't. The world of marketing always seems to be indefinite, loose, and unstructured. It seems like when people market, they don't really know what they are doing; they're just throwing things against the wall to see what sticks.

Not being a natural marketer frustrated me because I knew it was critical to success and because my biggest problem was not attracting enough customers. I could deliver a high-quality product, and I had the capacity to do more, but not enough people knew about DVD Your Memories, so the quality of my service was moot.

Tip: Become Capable in Everything

As I mentioned in the previous chapter, tailoring your product or service is essential to the success of your brand. Normally, we try to move toward our strengths. If we are good at something, we move into that field and we can excel. But this theory goes out the window if you are a startup business owner. The owner of a small business often becomes a jack (or jill) of all trades. You must be good at, or at least capable in, *everything*.

Some would say you can hire people to do the parts of the business you are not good at. But can you guess what happens when you hire someone for a skill you do not possess yourself? I'll save you the trouble—you get burned.

Within two weeks of reading *Think and Grow Rich*, a new idea burst from my subconscious and popped into my head. I realized what my advantage in the media transfer niche *really* was. I had been trying to compete with the other companies in my industry based on our product features being better. I would advertise things like *Free DVD Copy with Every Order* or *Custom Artwork for Video-to-DVD Transfers*. But these were small things. There was something *big* I was missing.

In the realm of search engine marketing, I realized that I was not competing with other local companies. Instead I was competing with the other companies that showed up in the Google search results—all of which were large national competitors, companies that were not local to San Diego. Yes, I did have features these companies didn't offer, but that wasn't making a difference to customers. My biggest advantage by far was that I was local and they were not. Sending one-of-a-kind memories through the mail was a fearful endeavor for most customers. With DVD Your Memories, nothing was put in the mail; everything was done in-house.

Just like when I convinced people walking into stores to like me and sign my petition within a couple seconds, the same timing applied to internet marketing. I had a couple seconds to differentiate the business in a way that customers preferred. And when I realized what it was, I changed my ad to read: *Don't Send Your Precious Memories by Mail. We're in San Diego, CA.*

And just like that, twice as many customers clicked through to my website.

I also changed the content of my website to further drive home the message that we were local. Within two months, revenue more than quadrupled! In April, I was struggling to eat and nearly going broke. By the end of May, I was earning more than $18,000 per month.

Tip: Find Small Ways to Enjoy Big Success

Suddenly having money after being broke nearly your whole life feels like you can finally breathe after holding your breath for years. Money had been the source of much stress and many problems that seemed to weigh me down. Now that the stress was gone, the weight I had grown up with was gone too.

Little things like buying popcorn at the movie theater made me feel accomplished, because I had never done so before. Going out with friends and not having to scan the menu for the cheapest item (and pretend that was what I wanted) was a freedom I had never felt. Filling my gas tank all the way almost blew my mind. I felt like the king of the world.

Your ways of celebrating will be different from mine, but make sure you pay attention when your financials move from red to black . . . and appreciate when they stay there! It's a major achievement for any business.

GROWTH BECOMES A MINOR HARDSHIP

By the summer of 2007, I had acquired the internet marketing chops and a new understanding of how to advertise unique competitive advantages. But more important, I realized the lessons from *Think and Grow Rich* were real. I was convinced that the business could attain limitless growth and there was no limit to my earning potential. This was the most valuable thing I had gained.

The next three months were a whirlwind. I kept getting orders at close to the same level as I did in May. Working on four times the number of orders I was used to was tough. I only had enough room in the office for one other person. The back office consisted of a hallway about six feet wide and fifteen feet long. At the far end was a small window that looked out to the small parking lot, and at the other end was one cubicle, which housed my new accounting computer. I had an editing computer, two slide scanning computers, and two video-to-DVD stations. The workstations were set up along both sides of the hallway.

I hired two part-timers, Tim and Amy, who would alternate working with me during the day. In the evenings, I had the place to myself. I loved having people around each day, but for some reason, nights were a magical time for me. I would push off the side of a desk like a speed skater and glide from workstation to workstation. At night, when everything was quiet, I could hear the prophetic sound of a jam about to happen in the slide scanner. I would be working on an editing project and simply slide over to pop the scanner and avoid the jam in less than two seconds. I got a lot done at night, and it felt good.

It took a few months to adapt to my new workload. By July, I was developing some bad habits. I was so excited about my work that sometimes I wouldn't take lunch. If I got hungry, I'd just grab a Coke from the vending machine. I was also so busy with orders—and so exhausted from my workload—that I stopped working out. Instead of energy from a workout, I relied on my excitement to push me through the day.

So it's no surprise that I gained some weight. Also, my right shoulder started to lock and pop, thanks to my right arm being stagnant in an awkward outstretched position for hours on end as my hand maneuvered the computer mouse.

But it was all worth it. Now I could save a few thousand dollars each month in order to invest in more equipment for the ever-expanding amount of work. I could even go out to dinner sometimes.

And then came August 2007.

DOUBLE THE QUADRUPLE

It had been almost a year since I'd moved into the law office. Summer vacations were nearly over, so people wanted their summer trips on DVD, just as Daniel and Victor had. And I was expecting business to pick up in September because of the upcoming holidays. But I was not prepared for my business to double again.

In August, I went from grossing $18,000 per month to $32,000. Orders were coming in faster than we could handle them. It didn't even cross my mind to decrease the pay-per-click marketing and slow things down. Shout-out to Amy and Tim, who were working late to get everything done.

I just remember feeling crazy, stressed, and excited all at the same time. I was meeting wealthier clients, and it was fun. One guy arrived in a Ferrari with his teenage son. I remember seeing him (or rather hearing him) park his car in the back parking lot. The car made a high whining noise I'd never heard before. As I was taking this man's order, I noticed the son using a phone I hadn't seen before. The kid told me it was this new phone made by Apple, called the iPhone.

Sometimes friends would come to meet me for dinner. I would do my best to pay attention to them, but if we were in the office, most of my attention was on the sounds of the office. We would chat for a bit about how things were going, and then I would always want to get the slide feeders filled up before we went to dinner and then perform the Non-Jamming Prayer over the scanner. Just before we left the office, my friends would take a trip to the bathroom. I would see them go around the corner and then come back after just a few seconds. The first few times this happened, I thought they were playing tricks on me. Later, I came to realize that my sense of time was skewed when I was working.

As we headed into the last quarter of 2007, I was determined to take on every order I could, no matter what. My resolve was tested one day when there was a gas leak on the street outside the office just as I was about to make one of the biggest sales of my career. Millie was an on-set teacher for child actors in Hollywood, and she had more than one hundred videotapes to convert to DVD. She said she wouldn't be in town long, and she wanted to drop them off at the office that day. Our building and entire street had been evacuated, but no way was I going to lose this order.

I could barely hear Millie over the emergency vehicles arriving outside my office and the high-pitched scream of the gas leak. Millie offered to bring the order back the next day, but I remember how adamant my old boss at the used car lot had been about not letting a customer hop on the "be-back bus." That's the bus that never comes back.

So I navigated what felt like a war zone, pushing my work cart through alleys and parking lots, and met Millie a couple blocks away from the chaos. We could barely hear each other over the whine of the gas leak, but in a few short minutes I had closed a big deal, made an about-face, and found a safe haven for Millie's footage until the coast was clear again on our street.

Despite my triumph that day, our business volume now required four full-time employees. I only had two full-time equivalents (FTEs), including me, in an office with about as many square feet as a bedroom. Something had to change.

OFFICE #2

I finally got a larger office in September 2007. The only criteria I had were that the rent be cheap and the space close to as many freeways as possible. I figured Kearny Mesa was a good area, since my current office was located there. I remember telling Tim that soon we could wave at each other from across a giant room rather than from eight feet away.

We were moving into the office space being vacated by 1-800-SAN-DIEGO, a directory company I had used many times in the past. The advent of Google put them out of business quickly, which was ironic because Google had allowed DVD Your Memories to grow just as quickly.

It was around this same time that I met Bryan Clark, who looked like a Nordic Viking with glasses. Bryan was working in the appliances section of my favorite electronics store. It seemed like I was always in there buying external hard drives, and Bryan's level of knowledge about anything technical impressed and delighted me. He not only knew all the specs for the hard drives I was purchasing, but also had recommendations about warranty periods and rates of returns. We just clicked.

Tech nerds weren't as chic in 2007 as they are today. We were still outcasts and didn't get much respect unless someone had an issue with their computer. When one of us finds a way to use those specific skills to do something special, other computer nerds can pick up on this energy. I think this is how Bryan and I connected so quickly. Mutual respect for each other's tech abilities isn't something that computer people instantly find at the top levels of a business.

Bryan noticed I was purchasing external hard drives all the time and asked me why. I explained a bit about my business and how fast it was growing. He gave me his resume, which was on a USB thumb drive he wore around his neck, and told me he was interested in working for me . . . even if it meant earning less money.

Bryan was exactly what the company needed, so while Amy and Tim helped with the office move, I hired Bryan and another full-timer named Danielle. Two half-timers and three full-time employees (including me) brought me to four FTEs, which is what I'd calculated the business needed.

Tip: Do Your Diligence on Every Hire

I felt confident about the time I had spent at the electronics store getting to know Bryan, so I hired him without an interview. But I was so frazzled when I interviewed Danielle, it went a little less formally than it should've. Interviewing Danielle consisted pretty much of me talking to her and telling her about all the cool stuff that was going on. I was so hyped up on the growth of DVD Your Memories, I forgot to make Danielle and her experience and interests the focus of the interview. A few months later, I had to let Danielle go when it became apparent she was not cut out for this type of job—something I would have known if I had stopped to actually listen to her.

Bryan worked in the videotape department. Danielle worked in image scanning with Amy, who was also taking orders and working on graphic design and our website. Tim managed our film transfer, worked with customers on custom editing and voice-over projects, and took orders. It was so cool to have five people in the office at the same time! We weren't breathing down each other's necks. There was room for everything.

A medium-sized dark mahogany desk with two chairs faced the front door. We placed a large conference room table to the left of the desk and surrounded it by oversized fake-leather executive chairs. We wanted this space to mimic a dining room so our customers would feel more at home. Then we placed some partitions so customers wouldn't see where all the magic happened, unless they wanted a tour.

With more room and more business, we increased the number of videotape transfer stations from two to four and then to seven by the end of the 2007. The image scanning department was increased from two stations to four as well. We hadn't yet started film transfer in-house, but there was a desk where the orders were organized.

Figure 5: Bryan Clark, my first full-time employee.

Figure 6: Bryan (right) with Tim McCaffrey (one of my part-time employees).

Figure 7: Bryan (left), Tim (center), and me (right).

Figure 8: Marily Benson (my mom) and me.

In superhero trilogies, my favorite movie is always the first one in which the hero answers the call and all the real growth happens. Maybe that is why I remember this time so fondly, even though not everything went as smoothly as it may sound.

MAYBE LIMITLESS GROWTH ISN'T SO GREAT

In April 2007, I was struggling to eat; by September, I was making as much money in a month as some people did in a year. I had a professional and proper office with legitimate W2 employees, tons of customers, and a marketing plan. By now, the business was able to accept credit card payments.

Don't get me wrong: It was tough—almost as tough as when I didn't have any business. I had employees doing most of the actual processing using our technology, but that was just one part of the work that needed to get done. I took most of the orders, handled the day-to-day bookkeeping, and managed the accounts payable and accounts receivable (although at the time I still didn't know that's what they were called). I also constantly adjusted the pay-per-click accounts, tried out many other forms of advertising (like magazines and newspapers), attended entrepreneur and trade conferences, spent my weekends at the farmers markets drumming up new business, and on and on and on. I was not qualified for the job, but somehow I managed.

And then the fires came blazing through San Diego.

The final week of October 2007 saw the worst fires in San Diego's history. Two days into the blaze, 500,000 people were evacuated from their homes—one in every six people living in San Diego County had to find shelter. The city shut down. Ashes were falling from an orange sky, and the freeways—usually jammed with traffic—were desolate. It was an eerie time.

After nearly a week of sweeping through the county, the fires had finally been contained and people's lives slowly resumed back to normal—except for mine. When residents fled their homes, they had time to grab only what was most valuable to them: family members, pets, and photo albums and other irreplaceable memories. Now, with the scars of the fires in their hearts—and in case of another natural disaster—people sought to preserve and protect their photos.

I almost feel guilty about how much business came in during that first week of November. We were doing as much business each day as we had done in an entire month prior to May. It was a whirlwind. I sometimes wouldn't leave the order-taking area from the moment we opened at 8:30 a.m. until about 3 p.m. By the end of November, we had totaled more than $70,000 of revenue for the month. It was completely nuts. I remember talking to Bryan late into the night as we were trying to get orders done, saying to him ominously, "Businesses don't grow this fast. This is crazy."

Unlike in May, we had no time to truly celebrate this fantastic growth, because there was so much work to do. I never had the requisite time to recover from the last double-up and office relocation in August before the crazy storm of holiday orders came in. I was beyond burned out and had no way to cope with the level of work and stress. That winter, I bought my first pack of cigarettes.

SHIT, MEET FAN

During those last two months of 2007, we made a lot of mistakes (besides the cigarettes—a habit that, thankfully, lasted only a year). But one error we made with a customer's order was the ultimate sin in our business: we lost a tape. The woman came in to the front office and cried and cried and yelled and got angry. This cycled for about three hours, but it felt like forever. That tragic event is about the only thing I vividly remember about November and December of that year.

Christmas Eve was the day all the holiday orders were due. The night before, we threw a company party at Seoul Korean BBQ. I rented a private karaoke room in the back where we all got drunk and sang bad versions of pop songs. Then Tim and I walked back to the office. Well, Tim walked and I stumbled. Tim worked well into the night, and I worked straight through until opening the next day to finish all the orders.

First thing in the morning, a lady came in. She had an editing order that we had been working on for over a month. It contained film and slides that we had scanned and compiled into an elaborate slideshow with titles, music, and so forth. When she saw her final slideshow, she was not happy.

She did a lot of editing work herself, and apparently we didn't get her instructions completed to her satisfaction. I was dead tired (and still a bit drunk), and her yelling kind of sounded like garbled anger, except for one thing that I heard loud and clear: "cluster fuck."

"Your company is screwed up," she said to me, her face going from a shade of red to dark purple. "You shouldn't be in business, especially with people's valuables!"

I stood there and took her verbal haranguing for the next twenty minutes. I couldn't argue with her, because she was at least partially correct. I hired and trained the employees. I created the systems (or lack of systems) that tracked the progress of each order. If something didn't work right, could I tell a customer that she needed to talk to someone else? I suppose I could, but who? Anyway, that was not how I wanted my company to operate. Someone had to take responsibility.

Shit, I realized. *It has to be me.*

Lesson Learned:
The Buck Stops with the Boss

I had barely learned to take responsibility for my own actions, and now I was being forced to take responsibility for other people and their actions. As I listened to this unhappy customer, I kept thinking: *I wasn't the one working on her order. Why is she mad at me?*

Then I thought about the tapes we had lost earlier in the month, and had the same reaction: *I wasn't the one who lost the videotapes. Why do I have to deal with all this crap? This is not my fault!*

My thoughts went on like this, wallowing in petulance, until I had a breakthrough: *This isn't my fault, but it is 100 percent my problem.*

That's the moment when I knew I finally had the attitude of a boss—not just a tech guy with a good idea.

The remainder of Christmas Eve was spent handling last-minute customers as they picked up their holiday orders. Finally, the day was done and the marathon year was over. I drove up the coast to San Jose, where I spent Christmas and the following three days sleeping.

CURSED WITH SUCCESS?

On the one hand, having DVD Your Memories take off was a dream come true. That's what every entrepreneur hopes for. On the other hand, at times I felt overwhelmed. I needed to find ways to keep running and growing my business—without going crazy.

Online Resources: Advanced Marketing Strategy & Hiring

Visit startuptosold.com for up-to-date resources on the following topics.

- Brand positioning/differentiation, unique selling proposition

- Early-growth strategy

- Easy way to set up new employee interviews

- Recommended HR tools to make hiring and onboarding easy

CHAPTER 6

HOW TO RUN A BUSINESS WITHOUT GOING CRAZY

What do you do when faced with a challenge you are not qualified or prepared for? How soon does your brain tell you to give up? Many years after these events I've described, when getting my MBA, one of my professors, Jim Olson, put the answer very eloquently: "There is only one difference between the top performers and the good performers—how they deal with adversity. Good performers will set lofty goals and achieve them if the adversity is not too great. But the highest performers will set lofty goals and achieve them no matter what comes their way."

No matter what comes their way . . .

Although I had yet to hear this bit of wisdom from Professor Olson, it was with this attitude that I set my sights on 2008.

THE STEEP LEARNING CURVE CONTINUES

Back then, when I had no idea what to do about something (which was nearly always the case), I'd find the top business books on the subject. Whatever business book I found at the time helped shape how DVD Your Memories eventually got built. And at the start of 2008, I needed to find a book on how to run a business without going crazy—or more specifically, how to set up a business to run itself.

Gabe, my Thailand travel buddy who had spent a weekend teaching me accounting the previous year, gave me the book *The E-Myth Revisited: Why Most Small Businesses Don't Work and What to Do About It* by Michael E. Gerber. It is not a book for business students; it is a book for people with a business.

Gerber, who is a small-business guru, uses an analogy of a technician (someone with expertise in a certain field) who starts a business, as is commonly the case. The technician does well if the company stays at a certain level, but as soon as the business grows, things spin out of control. That scenario was exactly what happened to me! I was a technician and handled everything fine—until we experienced exponential growth.

The book goes on to drop a bombshell insight: a technician is not the right person to run a business. Instead, writes Gerber, a company needs two additional positions: the manager and the entrepreneur. In fact, the technician is the one who performs the work. The entrepreneur is the visionary, the one who is always thinking ahead, coming up with new ideas. And the manager is the one who ties the two together, by creating and managing the procedures to get the work done in a controlled and systematic way.

But if the technician—usually the one who starts the company—doesn't up their game to realize the entrepreneurial and management work that is necessary, the company will go south quickly.

I felt that I was a great technician and entrepreneur, but I had not understood the role of management. So the most important lesson I learned at this time was that every business needs to create systems to run properly. You must get from working "in" the business (being a technician) to working "on" the business (being a manager). And that is what I set out to do.

Tip: Use a Franchise Mentality

Another concept in *The E-Myth Revisited*, called the "franchise prototype," describes an owner who creates a business as if they were building a franchise. Franchises succeed because each business replicates best-known practices: each store operates in a uniform way, following a protocol that is the same across the entire franchise. Even businesses with just one location benefit from having a franchise mentality because it reduces chaos and ensures consistency. That way, managers can focus more of their energy on managing the processes and systems, and less on managing the people.

EVERYTHING IS A LEARNING OPPORTUNITY

DVD Your Memories was closed from Christmas 2007 through New Year's Day 2008. And when we all got back to work in 2008, I had a meeting with Bryan. "If this company is going to be able to run on its own," I told him, "I can't be the one to run it." And then I asked if he would like to become the manager of DVD Your Memories. I wanted this transition to be finished by April, when I planned to take a ten-day vacation to Taiwan—my first real vacation since I began the company.

Bryan was the best candidate for the job. The first thing I asked him to do was read *The E-Myth* so we were on the same page. I was the entrepreneur, and he would be the manager, which meant we also needed someone to replace Bryan as the technician, filling his position in videotape transferring.

Enter Richard, a whip of a guy, just twenty-two years old. I saw his potential right away because he was so versatile. Besides his position as the videotape transfer technician, he helped other departments because he was a quick study, learning image scanning, film transfer, and editing over a few months.

Bryan and I mulled over the various aspects of the company for hours every day, as well as most nights. And something happened: we became two computer nerds who epitomized creativity.

Creativity isn't just reserved for artists. It is necessary in business and entrepreneurship. Let it be known, now and forever, that business is a creative process. We were creating the systems for a business model that had yet to exist, at least not that we could find. No one could tell us how to run the operation; we had to think outside the box when there wasn't even a box.

But unlike art, which has colors, shapes, and textures, business has the infinite complexity of the human condition. We had to sketch our customers, employees, and orders, and then add blocks of colors in the form of our machines, timelines, physical space, and technology. Ultimately, we were creating the perfect painting, one that would keep everyone happy and make money.

It took all my brainpower and then some, but experiencing unprecedented growth was a thousand times easier and more rewarding than dealing with a lack of customers. Bryan and I had worked for quite a few companies in our short lives, so we decided to incorporate everything good we had encountered at our previous jobs while taking the things we didn't agree with and turning them on their head.

For instance, one of our competitors was only a few blocks away.

We handled its overflow slide scanning business, and sometimes we would outsource to that company for our film transfer. The family that owned this business was friendly, and I liked them a lot. They treated their customers well, but they had this sign on the cash register that read: *Some of our DVDs may not be compatible with your DVD player. We are not responsible for compatibility issues.*

I remember seeing this sign and thinking it seemed out of character. It didn't go along with the impression I got from their company. They were nice people, and this sign would give customers a bad feeling; it wouldn't make them feel safe or secure. This is not to say the sign was inaccurate. At that time DVD compatibility was a problem. There was no recorded DVD that would work in all DVD players.

In one of our brainstorming sessions, Bryan and I discussed this sign and made a decision: the other company's disclaimer would become one of our differentiators. So we created a DVD Compatibility Guarantee—the only one in the industry at the time. If our DVD didn't work in customers' DVD players, we would buy them a new DVD player. This guarantee was plastered all over our marketing material and was part of our phone sales training. And in all the years I owned DVD Your Memories, we didn't have more than ten people ask us to purchase them a DVD player. It was a low-risk, low-cost branding strategy.

The time Bryan and I spent brainstorming the business was muddled with a lot of bad ideas, but even more great ones emerged. Our secret sauce was that we had a lot of task conflict (perceived disagreement about the best way to handle a task) but very little interpersonal conflict. In our case, the task was creating the systems that would make the company operate flawlessly, and there were hundreds of decisions to make. I would propose an idea, and Bryan would state his concerns. The key part, though—and something that Bryan has mentioned on several occasions—was that I listened to his point of view. I don't mean that I just heard his words; I also worked hard to understand his reasons.

We'd go back and forth, sometimes for hours, fine-tuning each detail of a system or policy. Eventually we'd end up with a decision or plan we were both happy with. I needed this consensus because as the manager, Bryan was the representative for the "workers" at DVD Your Memories. If he was not happy with the way the company was set up and run, then his attitude—no matter how hard he might try to hide it—would be obvious to everyone on the team. I wanted this company to run in the best way possible, a way that made sense. If someone asked us a question about *why* something was the way it was, both Bryan and I had to be able to explain it so everything added up. The answer would never be "That's just the way it is."

Tip: Revel in Disagreement, but Avoid Interpersonal Conflict

Interpersonal conflict is when two people don't like each other and cause each other trouble and frustration, usually by disagreeing based on personal reasons rather than the actual task at hand. This type of conflict is toxic and needs to be avoided at all costs.

Bryan and I would sometimes get into heated discussions that an outsider might assume was an interpersonal conflict, but that was never the case. The tension got too high at times, and we both needed to release some steam. Then we'd take a walk around the block together and talk about something else, usually the success we had been experiencing and how far we had come.

But ultimately we needed those high-intensity conversations, and I'm glad we both knew enough not to shy away from them. If Bryan had simply agreed with whatever I suggested or even picked his battles, we wouldn't have created a robust infrastructure for the company. Because we trusted that our "fights" were nothing of the sort, our relationship remained on solid ground, and just as important, DVD Your Memories ran well.

THE MYTH OF THE 100 PERCENT PERFECT PLAN

Everyone recognizes the need to develop a plan before they can execute on that plan. But deciding when you should switch over from planning to execution is a subtle point that's especially important when you're starting a business.

Execute before you're ready, and you're more likely to make mistakes that could doom your efforts. But plan for too long, and your startup won't be making changes fast enough to deliver on a product, or will get passed up by a competitor, or will simply lose momentum (particularly as you and your employees lose interest). Both extreme ends should be avoided. So how do you find a middle ground that allows you to make progress but minimize mistakes?

Try thinking of every plan as existing on a Perfection Scale from 0 to 100—0 is no plan at all, and 100 is an absolutely perfect plan. The trick, and one of the most important things I learned over time, was deciding which number means you should switch over from planning to action.

Here's how I plan that number.

I start with 80 percent. You can move this number up or down, based on how important it is you get a project right on the first try. Over time, I've learned that most of my 80 percent perfect plans are good enough to launch with—and I can always iterate from there.

Once I have a target number, I go into full researching, learning, and planning mode while being extremely mindful of my learning curve. While my rate of learning is high, I'll keep planning. Eventually the rate will slow down, when I'm learning less new information in the same amount of time. Again, it is of paramount importance to watch yourself here.

My success as an entrepreneur is tied to the speed I get to my target number. I have a bias toward action (as many entrepreneurs do) and am constantly being impatient with myself if I'm languishing in the planning phase. So when I reach the target number, then I can finally start implementing my plan.

CONTINUAL IMPROVEMENT CREATES SYSTEMS THAT STICK

As we created and tested our new systems for DVD Your Memories, our technicians were drawn to some protocols and not others. To Bryan and me, all the systems were important—otherwise we wouldn't have wasted our time creating them. But why did some systems stick while others were disregarded?

Here's the answer: If the perceived cost to use a system is greater than the perceived benefit from using it, eventually the system will not be used. The DVD Your Memories employees needed to understand why the systems we were creating were useful. If they understood the benefits, then they would use the systems. We hired employees who were purpose driven, and anyone who is motivated by a purpose will use systems if they are on board with that purpose.

Aside from communicating our systems' purpose, we needed to ensure the systems were simple and easy to use. Frustrating people becomes one of those "costs" mentioned above, so we set out to create systems that would be effortless.

When it came to creating systems that were both purposeful and easy to use, Bryan and I soon learned we couldn't make those decisions in a vacuum. We needed input from the people who would be using these systems on a day-to-day basis. Seeking their input served two purposes. First, listening to employees' suggestions made our systems better. Because the employees saw precisely how the systems affected their work, they were more than qualified to make great suggestions. Second, involving employees in the creative process gave them a say in how the company was being created. Because they knew good ideas would be implemented, they had an incentive to help improve the systems. They acted like owners instead of workers.

Those first four months of 2008 flew by. Things were changing all the time. I think we rotated each department around the office three different times, trying to find the perfect physical space for everything. No one else had grown a dedicated and local personal media transfer company on the scale we had (or at least we didn't know of anyone). There were a few national companies, but we were the only ones locally, with the ability to meet and talk to customers face-to-face. We were embarking on a road that no one had taken. And this was highly motivating for us.

TAKING CARE OF EMPLOYEES NO MATTER WHAT

Despite all the forward motion during those early months of 2008, there were about six weeks when sales started to slip. You can imagine my shock after the extraordinary and continuous growth we had in late 2007. I wasn't prepared to react or respond, because I was so focused on creating the systems. I thought back to the last time sales had taken a dip, in early 2007. It was such a horrible time, and I had to let a couple part-timers go because I couldn't afford to pay them. This time would be different. I had a great team, and I was determined to keep everyone on board.

One of the most important lessons that Bryan and I had learned about making a great company was that we needed to take care of the employees. So we promised the four other people in the office that when sales slipped, their hours would *not* be cut. Employees need to have consistency in their work life, and keeping pay stable is a big part of that.

When sales dipped, no one was told to go home early to save money. Instead we did everything we could do on short notice to push sales back up. Movement in the form of proactivity is key here. We just had everyone do something that could potentially lead to sales. I remember giving Amy a phone book and telling her to just start calling people. Everyone did something.

Such effort creates camaraderie and shows employees that we are all in this together. I was going to do right by them by not cutting hours, but they had to do their part. They all understood their role in keeping up momentum and how important it was.

I don't think many of our sales efforts led to anything significant, but the proactivity created energy. That energy lived in each person who worked at DVD Your Memories, and it said: *We will do whatever is necessary to stay afloat and make money.* I'm sure this energy had subconscious effects on our employees, and those effects were transmitted to the customers. Everyone could sense our level of commitment. And ultimately sales went back up.

THE BUSINESS DOESN'T FALTER WHILE I'M ON VACATION

By the time April 2008 came around, I think people who knew me well were betting against me taking my planned trip to Taiwan.

Well, I am happy to report that those people lost some good money. Not only did I take the trip and have a blast, but the business ran well without me, making as much money as it would've if I had stayed back and worked. That was a major milestone on my entrepreneurial journey: having confidence that the business could run effectively even when I wasn't directly involved each day.

After the trip, I returned to San Diego and realized I had more money in the bank than before I left! Being able to leave work, have it run perfectly, and come back to financial gains left me with an incredibly satisfying feeling. DVD Your Memories didn't need *me* to make it work; it worked on its own.

This was freeing. I was no longer tied to the day-to-day operations of the company, and that freedom allowed me to turn my mental space and energy toward creatively growing the company. In the great game of business, I had just leveled up. Now it was time to face the next challenge.

Online Resources: Systematizing Your Business (Franchise Prototype)

Visit startuptosold.com for up-to-date resources on the following topics.

- Best books for systematizing your business

- Free online tools for systematizing your business

CHAPTER 7

UPGRADING OUR BRANDING AND WEBSITE

One of the most important tasks for any business is figuring out how you're going to present yourself to the world. At DVD Your Memories, we needed to do more to develop our branding, including the structure and function of our website, which was amateurish at the time (I should know, as I designed it using a free template). Plus, our logo was outdated and not very memorable. That meant we were not putting our best foot forward when customers engaged with us.

So here's how we upgraded our branding and website.

GETTING THE RIGHT LOGO

Creating a logo was first on the to-do list. As always when I'm doing something totally new to me, first I read up on the subject and asked others about their opinions. Amy, my most tenured employee, was an amazing designer, and we spoke at length about what makes a good logo.

I also reread *The 22 Immutable Laws of Branding*, which reminded me of a few rules when it comes to creating a logo.

- First, the logo needs to be simple so it can be recalled in seconds. Who is going to remember a logo that is overly complex?

- Second, the logo needs to be versatile—meaning its color, details, and verbiage need to display clearly on a variety of formats: business cards, brochures, websites, letterhead, clothing. The more colors and complexity in the design, the harder it will be to maintain the integrity of the logo on these different formats.

- Third, the logo needs to convey (or at least be in congruence with) who you are and who the company is. For instance, if your company is fun and exciting, full of life and energy, and geared to a young consumer, you probably don't want a super professional, straightforward logo. IBM, for example, is a more B2B-oriented company, and that is what the logo conveys.

Figure 9: A simple, professional logo.

- Fourth, you have to be in sync with your audience. We didn't want to appear to contradict the values of our customers. Being out of sync is nothing less than miscommunicating, and customers will recognize this—sometimes unconsciously, but it will affect your business all the same.

LOGO IMPROVEMENT TAKE 1: A PROFESSIONAL SPIN

To help me implement these logo guidelines, one of the first things I did was hire a company to help create a new logo. The cost was around $1,000. The company had us fill out a form that challenged us to think about who we were and what type of company we wanted customers to see. We wanted the company to be fun and friendly, rather than dull and boring.

We were presented with six different options.

Figure 10: Our first professional logo options.

I liked option 3. It made me feel nostalgic, like seeing an old neon sign outside a movie theater. But then I realized that the design would not lend itself to being printed on clothing because of the small dots along the sides of logo. We learned a nice lesson and went back to the drawing board.

LOGO IMPROVEMENT TAKE 2: CROWDSOURCING

It's funny what you don't realize is available to you until you are in the market for something specific. When a friend told me about websites that host logo contests, I googled "logo contest," found a great online logo-design website called 99Designs, and set up a contest with a monetary prize of $150. Based on my direction, designers from around the world could opt in to create a logo that would appeal to me. The one I chose would receive the cash prize. In return, I would own all rights to the logo, plus receive the vector-based files so I could manipulate the logo to meet the needs of whatever merchandise or media I wanted to produce.

Although none of the designs submitted to the contest were "winners," we picked a winner anyway because someone deserved the prize money. Fortunately, this low-risk strategy didn't cost us too much, and we learned a lot in the process.

Amy, our image scanning tech and a budding graphic designer, was also busy working on designs. She designed a clever logo with an elephant that appealed to us. Why elephants? Because elephants never forget, and we helped our customers preserve their precious memories so they would never forget. But when we surveyed customers about this logo, they didn't recognize the symbolism.

A strong logo needs to be simple to understand, and when the customers didn't get it, we went back to the drawing board.

Figure 11: Amy's logo design.

Finally, we upped the ante and ran another logo contest via 99designs.com, this time increasing the prize to $450. More than forty designers around the globe competed to win. When we saw the logo from Indonesia, we were all sold. It was fun, friendly, and most important, conveyed the idea that we were dealing with personal media.

Figure 12: The winning logo.

CREATING AN EFFECTIVE, ENGAGING WEBSITE

Concurrently, we started designing a new website—a much more daunting task because websites are essential in today's marketplace.

If everything else works in a business, it's easy to overlook or forgive a bad logo. But websites are a critical arena for marketing and soliciting customers. Seventy-five percent of our customers found us through our website, thanks to Google AdWords. And customers were making their decision after visiting just two or three competing websites, so we needed ours to be simultaneously cutting-edge, professional, and friendly—a tough assignment.

We were clear on our differentiators: We were local, so people didn't have to worry about mailing their precious memories. We had a DVD compatibility guarantee. We specialized in media transfer rather than doing it on the side like other production companies. Now we needed to find a way to communicate these points visually and quickly, so people browsing sites could decide to call us in ten seconds or less, which is about the time it takes a person to make a decision about a company. The challenge became how to show what we were about—our mission, our core values, our personality—*and* highlight our advantages as succinctly as possible.

With this lofty goal, I cleared my desk (and my mind) and set out to construct the best website in our industry. Our old website was complete on a technical level, so I wrote down each important element from our current website on a small sticky note, noting what I wanted to retain.

Next, I googled "best of CSS websites" (CSS is a language used to describe the visual presentation of websites). I viewed hundreds of websites and copied down elements I thought we could possibly use, such as call-outs and slider bars that would organize the information displayed on our site.

Finally, I knew it was important that our website function in a way that reflected customer interests.

WHAT CUSTOMERS WANT FROM A WEBSITE

Contrary to what many business owners think, the intention behind a website is not to show off the business; it is to help persuade a customer to choose a business. This sounds subtle, but it is extremely important. As such, while creating your website, it's imperative to think like your customers.

Specifically, I wanted to present the information on the company website in the same order the customer would question our services, by answering their three biggest questions in order:

1. Can this company do the job?

2. What does the service cost?

3. How do I know I can trust this company?

We knew these were our customers' key questions because we were talking to hundreds, if not thousands, of customers every month. We answered their phone calls and met them in person. And as it turned out, going to farmers markets had also given me the advantage of meeting many prospective customers.

That market research was another reason we continued to work the farmers markets every week. Yes, it made us more money by bringing in clients, but it also served to test our ideas. And the method was familiar: talk to as many people as possible, listen carefully to their responses, and refine the idea (pitch) based on the new frame of reference.

It was the same approach I had used earlier in life to become great at getting political petitions signed.

Tip: Never Assume—Check with Your Customers!

I recognized that *thinking* I knew what customers wanted wasn't enough. Without asking them directly, I would be building a business based on presumption. Too many variables are stacked against small businesses already, so eliminating even one mistake could have a great impact.

We made sure to ask our customers for their input throughout this website-building process, and I've applied the same idea to many other aspects of the business. I have never regretted it.

DEVELOPING THE WEBSITE

I know only one thing about making a website: it was important enough that I should be involved in each step of the process. I made sure Bryan was involved with consumer research as well. With a clear picture in my head of what I liked and didn't like about other websites—along with the technical elements I wanted to retain—I looked on Craigslist for a website designer and came upon a college student named Rayan.

His resume was in the form of a website that was clean, concise, friendly, and accessible. That was the style I wanted our website to achieve, so hiring someone who had the same style seemed ideal. After talking with Rayan, I could tell he had the same entrepreneurial type of spirit as me. He was experimental and creative, and had the type of energy we needed.

Rayan worked with me through the rest of 2008. It took quite a few months and more than eighty revisions to get the website correct. The process was fun but also arduous, as we asked for input from every employee in the company and for feedback from our customers. As we built the website, here's how the three customer questions I described above came into play.

1. CAN THIS COMPANY DO THE JOB?

When we were almost to the finish line, I showed what I assumed to be the final version of the website to Tim, who was now one of the senior technicians. He pointed out something major that we might consider changing: the entire top portion of the Services page. My heart sank a little. I was ready to launch the site and didn't want to wait.

Tim explained that many customers weren't familiar with the exact type of media they had. For instance, to most people, movie film such as Super 8 looks nearly identical to regular 8mm. So how would they know to click on the Super 8 page? It had been decades since any of this media had been actively used, and many customers couldn't even name what they needed to have transferred.

Tim's fix was super easy—in fact, it was brilliant. We included a small icon of each media type at the top of the page, so customers would recognize the media they possessed. We didn't know it at the time, but that was the first time in our industry that this type of element was included in the navigational structure of a website. These days, it seems obvious, but at the time, it was a leap forward.

Sometimes the obvious things are overlooked. This is why taking the time to get into the head of your customer can propel a business ahead of its competition.

2. WHAT DOES IT COST?

Once customers know a business can do the job they are looking for, their very next question is the price. It may be hard to believe, but posting prices online was not the trend in the media transfer industry in 2008. Most competitors simply posted the services they offered and asked the customer to call for a quote. But calling for a quote wastes the customers' time by forcing them into a potentially lengthy and arduous sales call.

We realized that we were at the beginning stages of the information age, and savvy consumers were starting to expect to complete their research online and make their decisions with limited interaction with a salesperson. So we posted every price online along with costs for every upgrade we offered. We tried our best to make the cost as clear as possible, with nothing hidden. We wanted our potential consumers to easily determine and understand their cost.

We wanted to underscore that DVD Your Memories had nothing to hide.

3. HOW DO I KNOW I CAN TRUST THIS COMPANY?

Trust is important in every industry, but for personal media transfer it is especially important due to the nature of personal media. Our company was responsible for the irreplaceable personal memories of families. Customers would stand before us and trust us to transfer these memories for them, knowing that if we mishandled even one piece of media, it might be gone forever. We knew that the more we could be trusted, the more business we would have.

We spent a lot of time figuring out how to make ourselves trustworthy. We decided that the most important thing was to show who we were to our customers, because they couldn't trust someone they didn't know.

Normal relationships progress when one party becomes vulnerable to the other. If the revealing party is accepted by the other, then both feel more comfortable. The key was to show ourselves offering some personal information and displaying it on the website. So, when developing the website, we did two things with that in mind.

First, we made a descriptive About Us page that featured every employee who worked in the office. The technicians wrote a paragraph about themselves for the website, including something they were proud of and wanted others to know. We wanted to help customers feel they knew about us even before they made an appointment.

Second (another first in our industry, as far as we knew), we placed photos of department technicians on their corresponding service page. In that way, we could "introduce" the customer to the person responsible for handling their personal memories—while also illustrating our advantage of having one dedicated technician for every type of media.

When all was said and done, we were very proud of our website and all the work that went into it.

PROUD OF OUR BRAND

Our accomplishments now included a website that made sense to the customers, highlighted our competitive advantages, was easy to understand, and looked great. Not only was the end product better as a result, but the folks who helped provide ideas and were featured on the site had a hand in the future growth of the business. This, in turn, gave the employees a sense of ownership in the company. And when employees act as owners, that's when the magic happens.

I wanted the company to inspire and encourage our team to spend each and every day as owners, and the next phase of our rebuilding focused on just that: training, mission, and culture.

Online Resources: Logo and Website Resources

Visit startuptosold.com for up-to-date resources on the following topics.

- Logo design resources

- Web design resources

- Free website analytics tools

CHAPTER 8

A NERD CULTURE CLUB

By the middle of 2008—moving into our third year of business—DVD Your Memories now had effective systems in place, but there was still much to do. Anyone creating a business knows that your list of things to work on is infinitely long—and probably grows every day. Before I could grow the company further, we needed to cross off a lot of the items on this list.

IDENTIFYING OUR PRIMARY MISSION

We had created robust systems, but that was the mechanical, impersonal type of work a company does. Since employees and customers are not robots, we also needed to create the personal elements of our company. So we spent the remainder of the year defining our mission, vision, and core values, and becoming more deliberate about the kind of culture we needed to keep our customers happy.

Businesses are a combination of many moving parts, and when they all move in concert, the entire package makes sense to customers; they can't help but buy from you. With this in mind, providing people the ultimate customer experience became our primary mission, and that mission went way beyond the branding we had accomplished. What customers see in a logo and website are only one part of the picture. There needs to be a similar level of thought going toward the internal culture.

This viewpoint is supported by Louis V. Gerstner Jr., former CEO of IBM, who described culture in his book *Who Says Elephants Can't Dance?* by saying, "Until I came to IBM, I probably would have told you that culture was just one among several important elements in any organization's makeup and success—along with vision, strategy, marketing, financials, and the like . . . I came to see, in my time at IBM, that culture isn't just one aspect of the game; it is the game."

Company culture is notoriously difficult to define because it is created holistically. It is the personality of a business, the company environment, and the way employees and customers interact. It is the type of conversations the employees have, how good they feel when working and how they treat each other and the customers. It is everything, and it involves everyone. So it seemed right to take certain steps to make sure we maintained a fun, customer-focused culture.

Lesson Learned: Job Titles Matter

One part of our budding culture was finding ways to take pride in our work. This is where the idea of the "technician" was born. Instead of calling our people "employees" or "associates"—terms that are impersonal and lack specific description—we began to refer to them (and they referred to themselves and one another) as "technicians." As the *Collins Dictionary* defines it, "a person who is trained or skilled in the technicalities of a subject" more accurately depicted the nature of the work we were doing.

NERDS OF A FEATHER

At DVD Your Memories, we were all nerds. In fact, we hired people based on nerdiness. Our interviews consisted of playing computer games at a certain level of competency and answering questions about computer hardware. Bryan and I preferred the applicants who had experience with RTS (real-time strategy) games. Embracing our nerdy technician roles, we decided to wear lab coats when customers were in-house. Our "uniform" positioned us as "experts," and the intent was to gain immediate trust and authority. But those lab coats were not given out freely. New hires would need to earn the right to wear one. There were two reasons for this strategy.

First, I couldn't have the company represented by someone who was not yet up to standards. Before they earned the title "technician," new employees were required to go through a training period.

Second, when you work harder for something, you appreciate it more. We did not make the new hires work overly hard, but we did have certain standards they had to meet, such as getting to work on time, passing quizzes about the operations and history of the company, memorizing the intricacies of working with each media type, and being trained to handle customer phone calls and order taking. Once they met those standards, employees got a raise, a lab coat, and a name badge that indicated which type of media they were expert in.

Finally, as part of the company culture overhaul, Bryan and I finalized the "franchise prototype" manual recommended in *The*

E-Myth. We already had basic training in place—a description of how to do each type of job. Now we needed to write down what we, as a company, stood for—the core values of the business. We included it in a welcome guide to be read by every new hire.

Figure 13: Brandi Mitchell.

INSTILLING CULTURE FROM DAY 1

In the years that followed, I would meet with every new employee on their first day and explain our core values, the purpose and mission of DVD Your Memories, and the culture we worked within. Here is what I told them about our culture:

TRUST AND RESPONDING IN KIND

DVD Your Memories only works if there is trust on the part of the customer. This is due to the nature of the media we are dealing with. Our customers won't do business with us if they don't have trust in us. Therefore, we won't survive as a company if we don't have trust in each other.

I only hired employees I trusted. The very fact that they had gone through at least three rounds of interviews, usually lasting a combined four and a half hours, meant we had time to sufficiently vet them for character flaws. If we sniffed out any issues with honesty, that person would not be hired. I told each new employee, even before their first full day was finished, that I trusted them. I also let them know we left the cash box open during the day in case they desired to steal from the company.

Friends and fellow business owners asked me why I would tempt people with stealing. I have extreme faith in human beings, and I believe with all my heart that if you treat people with respect and honesty, they will respond in kind. I looked each employee in the eye, and with 100 percent conviction, told them that they were trusted here. And in all the stores and all the employees I've ever had, only once have I ever been proven wrong about this.

SHOW UP ON TIME AND TREAT YOUR JOB WITH RESPECT

At DVD Your Memories we have the attitude that working this job is optional. You can choose to work somewhere else. You could easily get a job somewhere else. And I could easily sell this business. But we are here, and if we are here, we are going to make the most of it.

I usually told new hires the story of my time selling cameras at the electronics store, specifically how the general manager didn't honor his promise to give me a raise. And then I talked about how afterward, I cheated the system. Again, I would look at the employee straight on and tell them I would go broke before I reneged on a promise I made. I was going to do right by them.

1% OUR FAULT = TAKE 100% RESPONSIBILITY

Everything we do at DVD Your Memories is guaranteed. Internally we have a rule that if something is 1% our fault, we take 100% responsibility. That means if we have screwed up just a little bit on an order, no matter what the customer does, we take responsibility and make it right. We never advertise this; it is an internal company policy. It lets everyone know that this work is important and that we stand behind our work and our process.

Explaining this policy to the employees on their first day really set the tone for their work. I also explained that in school, getting 99% on a test is amazing and something a student would be proud to achieve. At DVD Your Memories, unfortunately, 99% meant that we had scanned something incorrectly, and if a customer threw away the original media, their family treasure was lost forever. So our entire operation—workflow, training, and systems—was built with double-checks in place to catch even a single error. This put some necessary pressure on new employees to follow the systems and do their best, which, especially at the beginning of their tenure with us, was a really good thing.

It also gave new employees a choice: They could realize this job was not for them, and (thankfully) weed themselves out early. Or they could take our level of commitment to heart, join the ranks of other similarly minded technicians, and be proud of their position and the work they were doing.

NO SALESPEOPLE

The time of the pushy salesperson has passed. We have moved beyond the selling era and into the buying era. Everything is available online. People now scour the internet for information,

reviews, deals. It is very hard to hide if you are doing bad business. We do not have any sales positions at the company. Instead
we have technicians who are trained to understand the different
levels of quality.

Normally, when I explained this part of the company, the new
employee would breathe a sigh of relief. Most of the tech-savvy
individuals we hired had never done any type of sales and were
understandably apprehensive at the thought of needing to "sell." So
while I believe this policy was good for the customers, it also fit the
culture of our staff—even though some of those employees who
were apprehensive of sales later became our sales leaders.

EMPHASIZING A CUSTOMER FOCUS

When customers came in, they didn't see just any technician; they
were able to talk to the actual departmental technician for their
corresponding media type. This kind of access and partnership
is what customers wanted, and it underscored our differentiator.
Further, the company had none of the hidden charges so common in other companies. Every single price was listed in full on
our website.

Finally, we changed our training to include *Make friends with
the customer* as the top priority when going to the front desk to
take an order. We had a few tips and tricks to make this happen
quickly, such as matching the energy level of the customer, smiling
at them, mirroring, sharing a personal anecdote, and finding common interests.

Each of these changes allowed our customers to get to know
us more easily. After becoming friendly, we would earn their
trust by embodying the other core values of our business, such

as taking responsibility for any errors, offering all the guarantees, and so forth. It was an entirely holistic process that ended with the customer but contained our entire organization and started with the management.

LEADERS SET THE TONE

Throughout my years at DVD Your Memories, I wanted to be a better person because businesses reflect the personality and brains of an owner. If I became better, so would DVD Your Memories.

What is going well and what is going wrong can always be traced back to those at the top. Good things about an owner become the strengths of the business; conversely, if an owner is weak in one area, the business will be weak in the same area. If owners pay attention and are willing to see the good and the bad about what they have created, they will have the opportunity to go through what I like to call "smack-you-in-the-face therapy."

I call it that because the consequences of your personal rough edge will be reflected back to you in your business, whether you like it or not. It's not like you are seeking out a therapist, but you'll get that sort of feedback nonetheless. And the choice is yours: go the easy route and disregard it (usually blaming your business short-comings on others), or realize that everything happening in your company is a reflection of you and that building your business is an amazing opportunity to become better all around.

Why does a business mimic the personality of its owner? I believe it comes down to the complexity of daily interactions an owner will have with each employee and customer. Each of these interactions creates a trickle-down effect that infects every part of the organization. A blind spot in the development of someone at the top will create a hole or void in their organization. If there is something extra special about an owner, however, that differentiator will be undeniable.

This doesn't just go for owners; it holds true with managers at every level. Managers set the tone and influence the interactions experienced by their employees. Whatever that manager is responsible for managing—whether it be a department, a store, or a set of products—each area will be affected wholly based on the essence of who that manager really is.

All this culture and value training strengthened our team. Errors were plummeting, and the team was feeling good. Unfortunately, I didn't yet have all the leadership skills to let them know just how proud of them I was.

Tip: Have Leaders Interact with Customers

Seeking out customer input when making decisions about your business is critical, but in truth, the philosophy of connecting with customers went much deeper for me. I didn't go to business school, but I majored in psychology, and therefore human interaction was hammered into my head. This became handy when I was building DVD Your Memories.

As the business grew, I realized it was easy for management and owners to get far removed from the customers. I didn't want the responsibility for authentic customer connection to be left solely with our technicians, so we made it a policy that leaders at DVD Your Memories should have direct contact with customers. Even if it would be for one or two weeks a year, I made it my mission to have Bryan and I work on the ground level, directly with the customers we served.

THE IMPORTANCE OF PRAISE

To me, the team I had built was so obviously awesome that there was no need to point it out. I couldn't fathom the idea of the employees not knowing how highly I thought of them. Back then, I didn't realize how useful certain attributes—like having empathy, giving praise, and expressing gratitude—were for a business owner.

I don't remember who was the first person to tip me off that I needed to learn to praise the employees more, but I certainly can't forget how forthcoming Richard was on the issue. Being driven as I was, I lived in a zone that I had assumed everyone else was in, taking for granted that others were motivated by the success of the business, because that was what was motivating me. But managing people and leading a business don't work that way. People's paychecks are not enough to motivate and sustain them. We all want to matter and to do work that matters. Otherwise, apathy and depression—and worst of all, resentment—set in.

Once I was aware of it, I tried to turn my deep thinking toward this issue; after all, I had a college degree in psychology. It made me think about my first breakthrough with Timothy, the boy I tutored back in college. Ignoring his bad behavior, rather than acknowledging or praising it, had led to a decrease in the bad behavior. Now I was facing the opposite situation—good behavior—and it pained me to think that my team felt I was ignoring them. I needed to be doing the opposite of ignoring; I needed to learn how to give positive reinforcement.

What function does giving praise serve? How can we give it in a way that is effective? When is the right time to give it? I mulled over these questions and more. Part of the problem was that I had always been personally uncomfortable receiving praise. I didn't know what do to with it, so I would normally look down and feel awkward. This discomfort caused me to avoid praise altogether.

But now my overly humble personality would stunt the business unless I wrapped my head around this praise thing.

Reflecting on my own hang-ups with receiving praise, I realized it came from a belief that such praise wasn't coming from a place of authenticity. So I decided to make sure my praise was genuine.

If you give compliments but don't mean it, people can tell, and if they think you are ingenuous, they won't trust you. On the other hand, few things are as powerful as an authentic compliment given to someone who undoubtedly deserves it. When you share your gratitude or high opinion of another person, true connection happens, because in order to give genuine praise, you have to understand the person who is receiving it. You must find out what is unique and special about that person.

If you aren't accustomed to doling out praise (or receiving it), it takes some getting used to. After Richard gave me his two cents, I remember feeling a bit awkward the first time I purposely but genuinely gave praise to an employee. Over time, though, it became more natural to look at the person and see what amazing gifts they have that no one else notices. Chances are, they have worked very hard to become the unique, special person you are trying to see in them. And when you recognize their gift and let them know that you appreciate them for it, they will feel rewarded at a level beyond what money or status can bring.

Everyone has a unique gift, and I decided that as the boss, it was my job to figure out what each team member possessed that was special—and to build this practice into the company culture. Moving forward, DVD Your Memories developed a manager training module that encouraged the "work ego": the self-worth that a new employee develops in the first few days at a new job. Our managers were trained to find something special and unique in a new employee within the first couple of days—the earlier, the better. When they found that special factor, they let the employee know, but within earshot of the other technicians in the office.

Here is a fictional example: Heather, the store manager, walks over to the new employee and says to him just loud enough so the other technicians can hear it, "Dan, I know this is your first day, but I'm impressed by how well you listen to the instructions and advice from the other technicians who have been here longer. Many new employees try to impress the other technicians, but you have a refreshing sense of humility. It's really nice to have you here."

After being nervous all day long, Dan now feels great. His manager recognizes how patient and respectful he is trying to be since this is a new job. At his past jobs, Dan recalls becoming a little too eager to show off, and he has been really working on being humble. He hopes this will allow him to make friends and collaborate with his new coworkers.

Dan replies, "Sure thing."

Given his short response, it might seem like Dan is not taking to heart what Heather said. But Dan probably doesn't know what to say; he isn't used to getting commended in such a powerful way, and so early in his new work environment. We taught our managers not to take a terse response as an indication it didn't register, because it most certainly did. The things a boss says are always powerful, and they are remembered.

Dan will go home feeling good about his job. He will also work hard to keep the occasional praise coming from his boss.

We also found that giving a compliment is good for the managers as well as the office overall. We wanted our managers to remember that "catching" good behavior is at least as important as reacting to behavior that needs improvement. Far too many managers focus only on problems and neglect the positive things that are done every day. By acknowledging the positive things, managers help make the whole office more positive—something everyone wants in their work environment.

This is not the end of the story. There is another layer to praising people. Praise can be used not only to encourage and reinforce a behavior, but to change behavior. So, for example, say a technician is being defensive when confronted with constructive criticism. Instead of saying, "You need to be less defensive" (which, of course, will make them more defensive), you express your appreciation for how well they are responding to feedback, even the critical kind. Then you go on to explain how that is making your job easier and how it makes you feel good not to have to worry about offending him. Always mention the behavior and then how it made you feel—logic, then emotion.

If that employee is working even just slightly on this aspect of their personality, your praise will give them a massive amount of energy to keep going. You can't use this technique if it doesn't apply at all, but if it even applies 10 percent, it will be magnificently effective.

As I got better at finding the genius in others and praising them, they felt good, and in turn, I felt good. This kept my interest in continuing to learn about the psychology of praise from the perspectives of both the receiver and the giver. The things we focus on are the things we can master, and I was determined to master the secrets to a positive company culture.

CULTURE CAN BE SHAPED

What I learned from all these efforts is that although culture happens organically, it can still be shaped. And what shape it takes will largely depend on how you as a leader act toward your employees and customers—what you decide to emphasize, and what you choose to recognize and reward.

If you don't pay attention to the culture of your company, you'll end up with a hodgepodge of behavior that customers will perceive as inconsistent and perhaps even off-putting. If you do pay attention to culture, you can build a great workplace where employees will want to work (and hate to leave). What's more, you will build a business that customers will learn to trust.

Online Resources: Core Values, Culture, & Leadership

Visit startuptosold.com for up-to-date resources on the following topics.

- How to define your mission, vision, and core values

- How to create and promote culture

CHAPTER 9

AN OBSESSION WITH GROWING

An obsession, as defined by Oxford Languages, is "an idea or thought that continually preoccupies or intrudes on a person's mind." When it came to DVD Your Memories, I was the textbook example of obsessed.

Whether in my dreams, on the phone with friends or family, in the car on the way to work, or while attempting to zone out in front of the television, my mind played a self-written movie reel of scenarios that had to do with only one thing: the growth trajectory of the company—or more accurately, anything that would derail the growth trajectory of the company.

My business success was met with financial success. I was experiencing career life at a level above any of my close peers at the time. I was making as much money in a month as I used to make in a year, which of course was extremely satisfying. It is said that the high of making money mimics the high of cocaine. And just like cocaine is addictive, so is money. I felt amazing, and I wasn't reining that feeling in. Admittedly, I became a little full of myself.

As I learned, there's both an upside and a downside to becoming obsessed with your business.

THE UPSIDE OF OBSESSION

While thinking obsessively about a business may not be the same as actually working to improve one, I believe I mentally worked on DVD Your Memories between twelve and fourteen hours per day—and that was only my awake time.

The benefit of all this obsessive thinking was that I had prepared myself for disastrous situations. Like a doomsday prepper, I had worked out imaginary worst-case scenarios for everything. When an emergency popped up, as they do in business, I usually had a plan already in place.

I was also extremely focused on employees: finding the right ones, creating a work environment that was engaging, pinpointing the role that would best suit each new hire, and determining how the company could grow in line with the growth of these individuals.

The way I saw it, if my employees were growing, the company would grow as well.

Tasks and roles were changing rapidly and would continue to evolve as each employee evolved (and as I evolved). As amazing as my employees were, I knew I couldn't fit a round peg into a square hole; I needed to create the right types of jobs and environment for all of them, so they were happy and motivated at work. Turnover is always going to happen, but I didn't want it to become our culture.

As part of my employee obsession, I wanted to hire a bookkeeper whom I could rely on and retain for the long haul. I had come to the easy conclusion a long time ago that I was no accountant. While I knew it was critical to learn the gist of accounting, I needed someone who truly knew the ropes.

I had already been through a few bookkeepers; none had lasted more than a few months, all for different reasons. But when I hired

Brandi, I found a true gem. She became more than a bookkeeper; she was also someone who helped keep the business healthy with her positive energy and supportive personality.

Brandi knew how to have a healthy exchange, especially when she disagreed with something. A business can only grow with the perfect amount of pressure, and Brandi pushed back at the right times, with the right approach to disagreement. She was very good at being diplomatic while putting the pressure on others in terms of accountability and new ideas. In fact, Brandi was very good overall for DVD Your Memories and my goals for the business. Hiring her was one of the great things to come from my obsession with growing.

But there were downsides to that obsession, too.

Tip: Create an Environment Where Employees Can Speak Their Mind

What is the point of surrounding yourself with top staff—with creative and brilliant people—if they don't feel they can share their ideas safely, without harsh criticism or reprimand?

I will never forget Brandi's stance on our staff using the word "girl" when talking about a female over the age of eighteen. She made her case known: adult females should be referred to as "women" or "ladies," but not girls. After all, she pointed out, we don't call males over the age of eighteen "boys," so females should be treated the same. This made sense, and from then on the company made sure to use the appropriate term.

I admire those who stand up for what they believe in and who help make me a better person.

THE DOWNSIDE OF OBSESSION

One of the downsides of being obsessed with the business was that only two things could free me from my obsessive thoughts: when I became interested in something else or when I had enough to drink. And since true obsession implies that nothing else can wrestle its way into your consciousness, alcohol became my outlet.

At times even I would get sick of hearing myself talk about DVD Your Memories. So I would make myself a rum and Coke, with a nine-second pour of Bacardi Anejo or Captain Morgan, a can of Coke, and a ton of lime. Daniel had introduced me to this cocktail, also known as a Cuba Libre. A few of these would put me enough at ease that I could have dinner and play pool with my roommates without feeling guilty about not working—or compelled to work.

But quieting my mind like this meant paying the piper the next day. I wouldn't feel my best at work, and the lack of productivity caused a vicious cycle in my brain: first regret, followed by the panic of falling behind and having to make up for lost time. Whatever worries or thoughts I had put a cork in the night before came bubbling out with a vengeance the next day. If I engaged in some small talk or non-work-related conversation, I would look for immediate ways to get out of it or change the subject to a work matter.

Don't get me wrong: I tried my best to be interested in other people's stories or thoughts. But ultimately I perceived every interaction that wasn't focused on work as a waste of time and energy.

Another downside of my obsession was that, ironically, I started to forget things. This challenged me for quite a while. I work very fast, and when you go from task to task for hours on end, there is no way to keep each item in your head. I had always thought of this as a positive trait—being able to focus on accomplishing one thing after another, moving big projects forward. But it came with a disadvantage, too: I couldn't keep track of what I had said or to whom I'd said it.

And I got *really* frustrated when people would call me out on this. They would never tell me about how many things I *did* remember—only about when I forgot something. But the worst was that I didn't know whether I had said whatever thing they told me I'd said. It worried me. What if I became labeled as a guy who forgets things? Then anyone could just "remind" me at any time, and I would be powerless to disagree. I would just have to believe them.

I didn't like being at the mercy of other people or feeling like I was on the outskirts of some private joke, especially when I was supposed to be their leader. The only thing I could do about it was start writing everything down.

So if I had a conversation with some important elements, I would either make a note of the key points or email that person a summary. This method took a little bit of work, but it gave me back the confidence to run the organization.

Now, there were still times when I forgot things—or assumed I had told someone something that I hadn't. Thinking about work all the time meant being in my head all the time, which is like having a conversation that didn't actually happen. I'm sure there is some named disorder for this. On more than one occasion, this mysterious disorder came back to bite me—like when I wrote a message to Bryan and Richard about not doing what was necessary to get their bonus at the end of the previous quarter.

It was a short, slightly chastising message—not because I was upset, but because I had hundreds of other messages to write, and I didn't want to be bothered by requirements not being met. Bryan responded with an objection:

The system you refer to includes at least two items that were not
required last quarter. I am concerned because it seems like there
are things we (Richard and me) are expected to know that are
new without being given the information directly, and instead
they are referred to as if we already knew.

I started writing my own response to let him know that this
information had been available, and he just forgot to do it. As I was
writing the email, I checked my records (now that I was writing
things down) . . . and realized I had only told Brandi about the new
requirements, not Bryan or Richard.

Oops.

I was tempted to make excuses for myself; no one wants to show
that they made a mistake. But that is not what leaders do. Leaders
are honest about their own behavior. When they are wrong, they
apologize and do something about it.

Okay, I just checked my email, and it looks like I may not
have given you the 5 things needed for each quarter (and for
bonuses) until just today . . . I told Brandi since she emailed me
about it, and I must have thought I had already told you guys.
Okay, so I apologize.

So here is the deal: I'm going to have to work on more clear
communication . . . sometimes I think about the fact that I need
to tell you both something, but then forget to actually do it! ha!
Actually it really isn't that funny. And I need you (and Richard) to
let me know when there is something that is sitting uneasy with
you, or something that you think I can improve on. I will always
remember to keep my ego in check and put the needs of the
company first when I get criticism.

Obsession can be a good thing or a bad thing, depending on how much control it takes over your life. But one thing is for certain: while you are obsessed with growing a business and learning new things, the growing and learning won't stop.

TIME TO PROVE MY SUCCESS WASN'T A FLUKE

By late 2008, with Lehman Brothers making headlines and the economy in a tailspin, I knew I needed to make some further decisions. DVD Your Memories had quickly grown to be the dominant player in San Diego County. We were making great profit each month. Customers were happy and employees were happy. The systems that ran the business were nearly flawless, and there were few business-related fires for me to put out. Everyone was excited for the growth of the company. I was proud of our accomplishments.

So now what?

We could continue to run the San Diego office, and that would be fine. I could put a lot of money in the bank and give everyone big raises to boot. But I had this other, very exciting thought that played a big role in my obsession with the business: I wanted to know whether what had happened in San Diego was a fluke. Was I just in a perfect market at a perfect time, or did my business have legs?

Underneath my great feeling of accomplishment, something inside of me wanted to know if I could do it again. That meant opening another store.

I couldn't stop obsessing about growing, and a business can only grow as fast as the people running it. Luckily, I had enough awareness to know that my brain, like a muscle, needed a deep rest so we could all continue to grow. I needed to get away for a while in order to clear my head and consider the next stage. So I took a "think week" in Thailand.

I spent time alone in a bungalow, reading and thinking. I explored the island of Ko Pha-Ngan by scooter. And I meditated a lot on whether I had it in me to do it all again. What I discovered was that for me, it wasn't about not *wanting* to do it. It was about my aversion to risk.

During my time in Thailand, I thought about the many ways to grow a company, financially speaking. It costs a lot of money to grow a business. But I was scared to take on debt, so the only way I knew to grow was to use the profits from the previous year. In my case, I was already paying myself the minimum I could get away with ($30,000 per year) to save the maximum amount for growth. And to be honest, that was the company philosophy as well. We did not start any employee at a high wage. This allowed us to give bigger raises quarterly (to technicians) or yearly (to the manager). It also allowed the company to grow, which benefitted not only me but the employees as well. When a company grows, new positions open: managers move into executive roles, assistant managers move into manager roles, technicians move into assistant manager roles.

I also thought about how much to risk on that growth. I had always considered business to be like gambling. I didn't want to risk everything on the gamble of opening another store; I wasn't that confident. My plan was to put aside enough money from the 2008 profits so if the company went belly-up, I would have enough to live on for a few months. Since I didn't have a family depending on me, a house payment, or a car payment, the money I needed to live on was quite minimal.

By the end of the week on Pha-Ngan, I finally managed to stop my brain from obsessing. As this happened, I became grounded and attuned to myself, so I was truly able to listen to my heart as well as my head. Luckily, they were in concert, and they both told me it was time. It was time to expand the business. The energy was right to take on this new challenge.

IS THERE A RIGHT AMOUNT OF OBSESSION?

I wish there was a better way to grow a business than becoming obsessed with each part of it. But to this day, I don't rule out the correlation between the amount of thought you put into the health and well-being of a business and the actual success of that business—especially if you are a first-time business owner as I was.

I was fortunate that I didn't succumb too deeply to the downsides of obsession that I experienced. And allowing myself to really think long and hard about what I wanted to do with DVD Your Memories led to a clarity that ultimately paid off in continued success. So I'm not going to tell you to try to avoid becoming obsessed with your business. But please try to maintain a wider awareness beyond yourself and whatever preoccupies you, so you don't completely lose yourself in your obsession.

Online Resources: Founder Personal Coaching

Visit startuptosold.com for up-to-date resources on the following topics.

- How to deal with business obsession and other psychological headaches of being the owner/CEO

- How to use goal setting in business

- How to manage your health: regulating your diet, energy, and stress

CHAPTER 10

REALITY CHECK HALTS THE EXPANSION TRAIN

I returned from Thailand with big news for Bryan, Brandi, Richard, Tim, and the other technicians: we were going to take our model and copy it, opening a new location. The next logical place to do this was in Orange County, just north of San Diego.

PREPARING FOR THE NEXT STEP

I created some spreadsheets to forecast the revenue and profit I could expect from having two locations of DVD Your Memories. I liked what I saw.

The staff seemed to trust my new vision, and they were excited too. We were all proud of our accomplishments—and this time I remembered to tell them how proud I was of them, too. We recognized that growth for the business meant career growth for all of us.

One day in late 2008, when I was planning to purchase equipment for the impending Orange County store, Brandi asked whether I would consider offering health insurance to our employees. I told her that my new business coach had suggested I wasn't financially ready to offer a health insurance benefit—advice I did not question, especially when some friends said the same thing.

"How can you open another store and hire more people before you have taken care of the employees you already have?" Brandi asked me in her shoot-from-the-hip style. She was not afraid of my reaction. She had implemented an unofficial checks-and-balances system, and I liked it. I didn't quite know what to say, however, and I left the conversation feeling a bit uneasy.

As I mentioned previously, in business, as in life, you need to have people willing to tell you what they really think—but more important, you need to be willing to listen and seriously consider what is said. So it wasn't surprising to hear an objection to my plans from Brandi. She reminded me to practice some self-reflection, and that self-reflection changed the path of the business.

TAKING CARE OF EMPLOYEES

Because I didn't have an immediate answer for Brandi—and to be honest, because the question didn't make me feel good—I disregarded and buried the thought of her comment. To be honest, I was in greedy mode, enjoying the profit we were bringing in and enjoying even more the profit I expected to make with the new store. I was all too happy to save money by not paying into benefits.

But later that day, during my workout—right in the middle of a set of dumbbell curls—I had an epiphany. Sitting on the bench, slightly sweaty, I realized I felt guilty about something, but I couldn't put my finger on what. Then it hit me: *Brandi was right.*

I can't grow this business without taking care of the people who made it possible in the first place, I thought. *What a selfish, greedy son-of-a-bitch I am! I didn't start this company to take advantage of people for my own personal gain. I started it to find my own limits, explore the world, and have fun.*

I concluded that if I couldn't grow the business while taking care of those who made the success possible, then I wouldn't grow it at all. It was the technicians, the manager (Bryan), and the staff (Brandi and the other technicians) who made DVD Your Memories work so well. No matter how much genuine praise I learned to give them, denying health insurance was tantamount to telling them they didn't matter all that much.

If you care about something, I realized, you will take care of it. I needed to grow up and take care of my responsibilities—I needed to take care of my employees.

Being honest about my thought process and subsequent revelation was important to me. So I apologized to all the employees for my greed and for not considering how to support them and their futures.

I struggled for a long time with where I wanted to fit on the scale of business shrewdness. On one end of this scale is the super-nice guy who will bend over backward for everyone, keep working with employees who are not cutting it, and give everything to anyone who asks for it. On the other end is the business owner who doesn't treat employees well, gives out few raises, fires workers fast, and generally keeps a distance from employees for fear of getting too close. I had read books that espoused the benefits of each attitude. I had always thought my business would make more money if I took a more hardline approach to the company—for example, by not offering health insurance. But in truth, I leaned toward the nice-guy side of the scale.

When Brandi posed the health insurance question, she gave me an opportunity not only to be humble, but to be myself. More leaders should learn to be humble in this way, and maybe then more leaders would live fully as who they really are, even if that means naturally being a tyrant.

I was truly sorry for one thing above all: I had forgotten about my team. Now, in regaining the team, I needed to ensure them that they mattered.

There have been times in my life when I felt I didn't matter, and Brandi's challenge made me recall the lack of dignity I felt after my boss at the electronics store didn't give me the promotion he had promised me. I had learned from that experience that I wouldn't toy with people about anything—in particular, pay and benefits. I had worked hard back then, thinking I was going to receive a promotion in return. Brandi had reminded me that she and the others were working just as hard. I had to—*wanted to*— offer health insurance as a reward.

Ultimately, I realized that I needed the San Diego office to be running well, the team there to be happy, and the numbers to be solid before I could seriously work on expanding. I had already expanded before we were stable once, in 2007, and it amped up my problems. This time I would make sure our foundation was totally solid before scaling, and that meant offering health care insurance to our employees.

SETTING GOALS TO COUNTERACT UNCERTAINTY

Scaling is exciting, but it is also synonymous with uncertainty. This is especially true if you, like me, are not a naturally confident person. In business, there is no grade for you to receive at the end of each semester. There's no parent, mentor, or teacher who can tell you how you are doing.

But I wanted to know—no, I *needed* to know—how I was doing. I wanted to earn an A or even a B, and I wanted to know why I got the grade and what I could do to improve. Yet none of these measures or gauges are available to a business owner. Was this part of the cause of my obsession? Did simply not knowing my performance "grade" keep my brain working on the "problem"? Heck, Brandi's feedback about taking care of employees was the closest thing I got to a grade—and that was an F! Even so, I was happy to receive it so I could quickly do something about it.

Entrepreneurship is an individual sport, one that I was working harder at than anything I had committed to in the past. Unfortunately, you get so close to it, so deep in the woods, it is hard to get the view from above. I only knew that my growth rate was not at the levels of the entrepreneurs profiled in magazines I was reading, and my uncertainty increased with each comparison I made between me and those notable people.

For me, the solution to the problem of uncertainty and the insecurity that came along with it was to set goals. Only by having goals and being able to measure progress could I prove to myself and everyone else that the business was solid enough to support expansion.

I had two types of goals related to the business: short-term goals and long-term goals. Hitting those goals would take the place of any need for "grades." I figured that if I achieved my goals, I could give myself an A. And the faster I could get to those goals, the quicker I would feel a sense of security and acknowledge that I was doing a good job. This was important to me in order to sleep at night. With my own brand of empirical evidence for making the grade, I was able to release myself from taking my work home with me.

I created three short-term goals for the company:

1. The customers need to be happy.

2. The employees need to be happy.

3. We need to make money.

Goals floating around in my head were never going to be as important, however, as numbers I could track with my eye. So I used Google Sheets—although Excel could've worked just as well—to get them down on "paper."

I wanted my goals to be as real and tangible as possible, so getting them out of my head and into the world, where I could be accountable for them, was imperative. Using conditional formatting to color-code our metrics turned out to be extremely useful. We used green shading for numbers that were in the "good" category, yellow for numbers that were slightly below standards, and red for numbers that were unacceptable. With color coding, the spreadsheet became an at-a-glance barometer of the company's health.

Tip: Share the Numbers with Employees

A benefit of the color-coded system I developed was that it enabled me to share the numbers with my employees. I imagined that my employees would appreciate having a sense of what was important to me, as the owner—and I was right.

When their scores were good, Bryan was proud and praised the team for a job well done. Conversely, the employees could also gauge anything not in the green as something they could foresee needing a conversation about, and the warning helped them prepare for it. Many times, people on the team began to problem-solve before I could even think about how to solve it myself.

If you're reluctant to share a progress sheet with employees, I'd still recommend at least sharing this information with managers or supervisors. The more information they have about how your business is doing, the better they will be positioned to make decisions that will take you closer to the company's goals.

To populate this spreadsheet, my business coach introduced me to the concept of key performance indicators, or KPIs. This became my metric—my measurement of whether I was achieving my goals or not.

To begin measuring my first short-term goal—*The customers need to be happy*—we created a survey using Survey Monkey, one of the original online survey tools. There were only a few questions, because we thought the customers would avoid completing a longer survey. Using a scale of 1–5, our questions ranged from asking what customers liked about our product/service and what they didn't like, to their opinions on the conduct of a technician and satisfaction with quality. I followed the survey over a few months' time until we had at least thirty responses (for statistical significance reasons).

I decided that 4.6 out of 5 was an indication that customers were indeed happy. Anything below that would mean we needed to work to improve customer satisfaction. Additionally, knowing which technician had provided customer service and which technician had fulfilled a respective order were helpful in determining whether I reinforced with praise or, if necessary, provided further training to an employee.

To assess my second immediate goal—*The employees need to be happy*—I implemented an anonymous survey within the office, devising questions like "Would you recommend this job to a friend?" and "Compared to your last job, how satisfied are you at DVD Your Memories?" I also asked an open-ended question so employees could provide additional information and suggestions if they desired.

I had been so focused on asking the right questions in these two surveys that I forgot to consider how I would feel after reading the answers! Honesty is not always pretty. A small percentage of employees had negative responses, and those were hard for me to swallow. Some employees will just never be happy, I figured. But even knowing this, I still couldn't get over some of the comments I received over the years.

Overall, though, I received much more positive feedback and suggestions from employees than bad ones. Some of the suggestions we experimented with were technician parties, company contests, storewide lunches to reward good performance, profit sharing, more time off, and other benefits.

The final short-term goal was something more quantifiable: *We need to make money.* To determine when we met this target, I used the total net profit based on our profit-and-loss statement (also known as a P&L or income statement). I like to use the P&L because it takes out anything purchased for growth, such as new equipment, as this new equipment would be considered an asset and not an expense.

I chose a monthly revenue number that made me feel good— and I stuck to it. Striving to meet these three short-term goals—and succeeding!—provided a much-needed feeling of security and completeness, and that helped curb my obsessive thoughts.

READY FOR THE NEXT STEP

My long-term goals were all related to growth. I wanted them to be goals that my entire staff, especially the key players, could get behind, get excited about, and be inspired to accomplish.

My central longer-term goal, as I mentioned before, was to open a store in Orange County. And once I had the numbers—in the form of the short-term goals—to prove that the San Diego location was on firm ground, I finally felt ready for the next step.

Online Resources: Advanced HR Resources

Visit startuptosold.com for up-to-date resources on the following topics.

- HR benefits and policies

- Employee and customer surveys

CHAPTER 11

THE 1ST SECOND STORE

One of the main reasons for pursuing a second store was simple: I wanted to see if we could replicate the success we had experienced in San Diego. I knew of no other personal media transfer company that had two local stores.

Plus, the San Diego store was self-sustaining: Bryan had been doing a fantastic job as manager, the technicians were all well-trained, and our customers were beyond satisfied. Brandi was handling all the financial, legal, and tax matters—to name just a few things. My spreadsheet was in bright green, and I was feeling supported and ready for expansion.

It was time to put my ambitions to the test.

PEOPLE ARE PARAMOUNT

When the idea of opening a store in Orange County began to take shape, much of my thought process was dedicated to which roles each employee would move into. If I didn't have the right team, the expansion to OC was not going to work. Fortunately, when I spoke to my staff about opening a second store—something that

I didn't think had been done before—they were nearly as enthusiastic as I was.

I knew I needed to create this growth based on the people I already employed, the skills they possessed, and the natural desire for their own career growth. This was a team effort, a symbiotic relationship, and I needed their support. If I left the staff out of the loop when it came to making big decisions, they might feel alienated and resentful. The alternative was to bring them into the decision-making process to help define how the company would grow and how each of them could contribute.

It had to be a collective dream.

My plan was to live in Orange County for several months until I felt the OC store was stable on its own. But for that to happen, I needed a manager to be there, too. The new manager position in OC was going to be one of the most important positions the company would ever fill. If we hired the wrong person, the OC store would not take off, and we might get discouraged and stop there. If we hired the right person, the store could flourish and the profits could fund future expansion.

Tip: Promote from Within

When it comes to key positions like managing a newly opened store, I remain adamant to this day about promoting from within. Insiders not only can do the job, but also are keepers of the culture—something that is increasingly important as the company expands.

In my opinion, for key positions like this, it is better to promote from within than to hire from outside the company. Richard was the most competent technician at the San Diego store. He had a constant thirst for learning and would finish his work quickly and then browse the internet. This type of employee can be frustrating for many managers. Someone who is highly capable and gets bored easily is hard to manage. It is easier to have a technician who operates at the same pace as others, gets their work done in an orderly fashion, and doesn't need too much attention. Richard was exactly the opposite, and I knew if I didn't challenge him, I'd lose him—and I didn't want that to happen.

By the end of 2008, Richard had worked in each of the other departments, because he had the time and the brains. He was like a sponge, soaking up all the knowledge of the company. Who better to open up and manage the new OC store than Richard? (In fact, his ability to learn all the departmental roles contributed to our later decision that all managers should be trained in every department in order to manage each one more empathetically and effectively.)

I've always made it a point to surround myself with trusted friends and colleagues who have talents and abilities. Every single person I know is a genius in a certain area—their own X-Men ability—and I've always felt it was my job to recognize the genius that surrounds me on a daily basis. So how do I recognize genius?

One of my first life lessons came from wrestling. I started wrestling in fourth grade, and by middle school I was breaking school records. But no matter how good I was, there was always someone who could beat me. I had to get comfortable with the fact that I was not the best at *everything*.

This lesson continued in sixth grade, when I went to middle school early with a special class for gifted and talented education (GATE). In elementary school, I had always been one of the smartest kids in certain subjects, but when I got to the GATE class, I saw what true genius was. My friends in the GATE class were taking advanced algebra, picking up languages nearly instantly, writing with perfect grammar, and even building computers. In our small class, I quickly sobered to the fact that I wasn't the best at *anything*.

The point is, if you have a mindset that you must be the best at everything, then your brain will not allow you to see others who shine brighter than you in one area or another. I didn't want to spend my energy constantly looking for ways to outshine others; on the contrary, I wanted to hire people who would shine brighter than me and keep my ego in check. So now I purposely seek out others who can beat me—not literally beat me, like in wrestling, but simply have more skill in some specific area.

Tip: Acknowledge Talent When You See It in Action

As I became more comfortable being surrounded by people who were more talented than me in some areas, I learned that instead of turning my eyes down when I see them doing something incredible and impressive, I need to raise my head up, look them in the eyes, and show them that I truly see them—that I recognize them and their talents.

The simple act of publicly recognizing someone else for their genius is one of my top leadership tips, as it has so many positive benefits. First and foremost, it shows that I am strong enough to recognize someone who is stronger. This is powerful.

Recognizing a talent in someone also engenders positive emotions in them. It makes them feel good, and they link that good feeling to you. Now you are someone who can give them proud feelings. They will be happy not only to see you in the future, but to show you those talents again and again. When you find a task that is particularly suited for them, you will be able to ask them for help, and they will most certainly oblige.

PREPARING FOR EXPANSION

The 2008 holidays were great. We made a lot of money and turned our breakroom/accounting room into a floor-to-ceiling storage closet for all the boxes of equipment and stock purchased for the OC store—even though we hadn't chosen a store location yet. There were tax benefits to this approach: anything under a certain dollar amount (depending on your industry) can be written off as an expense in the same year, so we could expense smaller items in 2008. If those same items were purchased in 2009, we would have had to pay taxes on the money that was allocated for purchasing them, which in effect made those items much more expensive.

Once the busy holiday rush of 2008 was over, however, the hunt for office space began. We opted for an office in Costa Mesa, a coastal city on the western edge of Orange County but in the middle vertically (north-south). We got a fine deal on a two-story office near the coast, off State Route 55. The bottom floor was for taking orders and editing. The top floor consisted of one large room and contained all the transferring equipment.

I also found a great two-bedroom apartment for Richard and me—now both coworkers and roommates. We were ready to roll!

Still operating on a shoestring budget, we moved all the equipment we'd purchased from the top floor of the San Diego office down to the giant U-Haul truck ourselves. Then we drove from San Diego to Costa Mesa and moved everything into the new OC office. The move was fun and exciting. I remember Bryan taking a 230-pound Gorilla Rack up the outside stairs all by himself, and hiding a beer in the ceiling when we all got drunk together after moving in—something that would become a small part of the culture going forward.

A couple of good friends, Gabe and Marques, even drove to OC to help with the move. When we were finished, we all went to In-N-Out Burger. Richard and I spent the next couple of weeks setting up everything that goes into opening a new store, from building desks to making sure phone lines were working to testing internet speeds.

Finally, on March 9, 2009, I sent an email to the staff outlining how the two stores would be coordinating their operations and communication. And we were ready to launch.

LAUNCH!

Once we were ready for business, we turned on our internet marketing ads through Google AdWords and received our first order that same day. Within five to six weeks, the OC store was sustaining itself, and soon thereafter it began to make money.

Living with Richard turned out to be a great experience. We would work hard all day and then come back to the apartment around the same time and work out together, either playing tennis or going to the gym. After dinner, we would go to the hot tub and chat—usually about business. During this time, I became friends with Richard, which business owners typically try not to do. We played video games, talked about dating and women, and went out to bars together. I think Richard even saw me dance once when I was overly intoxicated.

As a coworker and new manager, Richard grew a lot during this time. Only one time did our friendship become awkward: when I noticed Richard was consistently late to open the store. When it was still just the two of us running the store, I told Richard that even though he was only a few minutes late, and we didn't have many customers at that time, tardiness was unacceptable by the company standards.

"If you want to be a store manager," I told him, "you cannot be late." In fact, it was important for him to be there early so he was prepared for any customers who might be waiting when we opened.

Richard rallied, and I was so impressed. He had uprooted his life to move to OC and was all in, doing whatever it took to learn and grow. Richard was challenged with running every aspect of the Orange County store, handling four out of five departments simultaneously by himself—videotapes, film transfer, editing, and audio transfer—and taking most of the orders. He was doing the work of three technicians; plus, he was managing the store. It was a lot to ask of him, but he handled it. Working with Richard during those months showed me what he was made of. He showed me that I could trust him to handle the store after I was gone.

A fortunate, unforeseen camaraderie was born between the two store managers, Richard and Bryan. They made friendly bets for a case of beer: the store that earned more money bought the other store a case of beer. During those first few months, the OC store was small, and Richard had a lot of beers to drink. The two managers worked together well. Bryan could commiserate with Richard about being a manager and help Richard with technology issues.

Over the course of a few months, the OC store was making enough money for Richard, who was now an official manager, to hire his first employee. This was no small task. Knowing how to handle employees, how friendly (or strict) to be, and the philosophy behind the training were all important elements that Richard and I would have to learn.

After hiring a few employees, the OC store gained momentum and energy. With both stores fully staffed, we turned our attention to maintaining the company philosophy of having fun. As a way to bring the staff together for bonding and team building, we introduced quarterly parties. Why go through all the trouble of building a company, I figured, and not bring everyone together as friends to drink and play multiplayer Unreal Tournament or Halo?

I allotted thirty dollars per employee per store per quarter to spend on each celebration. The store could choose to do anything it wanted, so long as nobody was excluded and the activity was legal. The San Diego office chose to do things like bowling and go-karts. Orange County had a lot of LAN (local area network) parties, where each person would grab a computer in the office and play a computer game together. No one was required to attend a party, but it was encouraged. Significant others and friends were almost always welcome. Sometimes employees from the other store would drive up or down to go to the parties, too.

A side benefit of these parties was that employees got to know each other on a more personal level. When they got back to work on Monday, they could chat about Saturday night—who got *owned* (gamer-speak for "completely dominated") or whatever else happened. This brought each team closer together and greatly enhanced employee job satisfaction and our company culture.

Lesson Learned:
Be Serious with Onboarding

We made a mistake in OC by inviting a brand-new employee to a company party. He saw all of us cutting loose, getting drunk and rowdy with each other. It was a fun night, but when Monday came around, the new person was still in goofing-off mode. We didn't realize what was going on; we just thought that this new employee was not serious about work. But it was not his fault—it was ours.

We failed this employee because we didn't understand the significance of first impressions. After that, we learned to always treat the company with 100 percent seriousness when on-boarding new employees, so their brain would be wired to have this respect for the business. Only after they had earned *our* respect through hard work and proved themselves to the company would they be invited to the parties. And then they would feel like they'd earned it.

A BIG OPPORTUNITY FOR OC

Richard was working through the fun and challenge of running a new store. The Orange County location was making money, but not all that much. The San Diego store had grown much faster, and we didn't know why. But we kept working at our marketing mix and keeping our customers happy. We figured it would only be a matter of time before our hard work would pay off.

Then we heard about a request for proposal (RFP) that the City of Irvine (next door to Costa Mesa) was initiating. I didn't know what an RFP meant at the time, but quickly learned that it was a bidding process for a large contract. The city wanted to convert its old city council meeting recordings from as far back as the 1970s, on various types of media. There were more than a hundred boxes of VHS tapes, audiocassettes, and quarter-inch reel-to-reel audio tapes.

We felt we were poised to win this contract because we were not only local, but also the most equipped company to handle this volume. Most other media transfer companies were either mom-and-pop operations that did this type of work out of their homes, or video production companies doing the work on the side. We were a company built to handle media and only media. We had one full-time employee in each department who worked solely on each type of media. We were true specialists. This had allowed us to become experts in each media type as well as have the capacity to handle large orders.

Brandi spearheaded the project, and the entire team worked hard on our proposal. Richard, Bryan, and I gathered all the data that we would eventually use. It took at least a month to complete the proposal. We went to meet the city workers in charge of the project to get a firsthand look at the media. We also created custom graphics for their DVDs. Then we priced the project on the low end of the scale, but not so low that we wouldn't make any money. In total our quote was over $40,000—about double the amount of money the OC store was making each month. We figured the job would take us a few months from start to finish.

I was still working in the Orange County store when the phone rang. Richard and some other technicians saw the caller ID was from the City of Irvine, and they stood at the top of the stairs to listen in.

"So, when can you pick up the materials?" the woman asked me.

I was so nervous I couldn't think straight. "Does this mean we got the order?" I asked.

She confirmed, as if I should have already known. Our bid had won.

I was not expecting the joy that followed my announcement to Richard and the others. We ended up holding each other's shoulders in a circle, cheering, and jumping up and down! This was exactly what Richard's store needed to infuse some energy—and dollars.

The feeling of a job well done is great, but sharing it with people you not only work with but genuinely care about—that feeling is amazing.

PLANNING FOR THE UNKNOWN

The next few weeks were spent getting ready. Since the order was so large and needed to be completed in only a few months, we would have to purchase new equipment and hire someone dedicated to just this job.

Media transfer requires that you record most media by playing it back in real time, so an extended-play, six-hour VHS tape takes six hours to record. Encoding it and burning it onto an archival DVD comes next, followed by printing and labeling the DVD correctly. One tape can easily take an entire day to complete. So the way we make money as a company is by scale: we run multiple decks simultaneously.

But how could we know how much new equipment to purchase or how many employees to put on the project? This is where I turned once again to a friend with extreme talent: Gabe, who first taught me about accounting practices. Gabe could navigate and type in Excel without even using a mouse—and fast. I had an idea about how many stations we needed to set up, but Gabe had a way of creating a spreadsheet that solved for the thousands of combinations, to give us the most profitable way to complete this order in the least amount of time.

With more employees, we could get the work done faster, but that would add hourly cost. With fewer employees, we would need to purchase more machines. This was easy to understand, but figuring out the number of machines we needed was more difficult, since each of the three media types was different in quantity, run time, and burn time.

Gabe's spreadsheet solved for all this using the solver add-on function for Excel. Essentially, you can choose a cell to solve for, making it the lowest possible or the highest possible number. And then you select cells that are your variables—those that the function can modify endlessly until it finds the combination that gives you the best possible result—similar to linear programming. In our case, the number of employees and the number of machines were the variables, and the total was calculated into a final cost over many months, which was the result that we were solving for. Gabe's solution was genius and saved us a couple thousand dollars.

I had learned my lesson by then and made sure to acknowledge Gabe's contributions. Just like praise, recognizing talent must be genuine. If Gabe thought I was simply impressed with his Excel skills for the sole purpose of using him for that skill, it would backfire. I would be "using" him. If you go around looking to use people, you will be discovered as inauthentic, and your staff will not trust you.

Tip: Pay People What They Are Worth

I did not pay Gabe the first time he came down to San Diego to teach me accounting. But once I started to make money with the company, I made sure that he was paid. And I never negotiated him down from his wage. Sometimes, when I truly valued the service, I offered more than the person asked.

Like me, you may not be able to pay full wages to everyone who helps you at the beginning. But once you can afford it, offer to pay the people who are doing work for you, even if they are friends. Friends will not want to overcharge you, but if they are doing work that takes time, then you need to offer to pay them. It shows that you value them.

UP AND RUNNING

With Gabe's help in planning out exactly what we needed, I felt comfortable that we had what it would take to operate the OC store successfully. The reality of running two stores, however, hit me a little harder than I had anticipated.

Online Resources: Scaling and Growth

Visit startuptosold.com for up-to-date resources on the following topics.

- How to build consensus

- Team strength finding

- Optimizing system build-out for maximum profitability

CHAPTER 12

IMPROVING THE ABILITY TO GET THINGS DONE

B y the summer of 2009, a few months after the Orange County store launched, I noticed how much busier I was with two stores to manage instead of one. Even with strong managers and a lot of help from Brandi, there was more on my plate than ever.

The amount of headaches for business owners or managers is related to how many employees, customers, and physical locations they have, and my workload had effectively doubled over the previous few months. When it came to my duties, I was starting to feel like I was always underwater. More and more emails came in, and more personnel problems, equipment issues, lease concerns, special projects, and marketing opportunities emerged. I needed a way to handle all this new work.

As a result, for the rest of 2009, a lot of my attention was focused on improving my own skills in several areas so I could continue to be an asset to the business without getting burned out.

LEARNING HOW TO MANAGE MY ENERGY

For two months in the late summer of 2009, I focused my attention on learning how to be more efficient with my time. I read books and blogs, followed websites like Lifehacker.com, experimented with new software—anything I could get my hands on to find out how to handle running two stores without getting stressed out. In the end, most of what I learned came from a book called *Getting Things Done* by David Allen.

The most important thing I learned was that the brain cannot stratify to-do items based on when they are due. Anything the brain remembers is of equal importance, and it will continually remind you of all those things. When the number of items you keep in the brain feels too large, then you feel stressed and overwhelmed.

Imagine a graph with two bars, and each could be filled up between 0 percent and 100 percent. One bar is your energy, and the other is your current to-do list. When the to-do bar grows higher than your energy bar, you feel stressed. You don't have the energy to deal with the workload. But when your energy bar is higher than your to-do bar, you feel like you can handle the workload. Remember, the same workload can feel either overwhelming or manageable, depending on your energy level.

This is like RAM (random-access memory) in a computer. There is only so much space available in RAM, and when it gets filled up, your computer starts running slow. Luckily, there is a way to get to-do list items out of the RAM. This is what David Allen's Getting Things Done˚ (GTD) system is all about.

GTD is all about getting things out of your head and into a system. When an item goes into that system, the brain trusts that it will get done and can stop thinking about it. Then you just follow your system, and the brain can be clear. I won't go deep into the system here, but I recommend any version of David Allen's seminal book.

What I noticed about myself is that the amount I could hold in my brain without feeling stressed was related to my energy level that day. If I felt worn down or tired, I would be able to manage only a fraction of my workload compared with when I felt energized. So the first thing I focused on was maintaining a high energy level.

For me this meant I had to start paying attention to my diet, sleep quantity and quality, and daily exercise. I started getting back to the raw food diet I had dabbled in when I was in college. I remember that lifestyle gave me the most energy I had ever felt since I was a kid. Next, I aimed to get at least seven hours of sleep. And finally, I committed to working out every day or at a minimum every other day. With more energy, I noticed a reduction in the feelings of stress.

After learning the GTD system and implementing the other healthy changes into my work life, everything changed. I was relatively stress-free, even with the doubled workload. If I hadn't gone through this process of systematizing my work, I'm sure I would've been forever stuck in an endless workstream. The process was so effective, I even included the system I adapted for my life into the manager's handbook.

Lesson Learned: High Energy Has a Ripple Effect

My increased energy helped sustain good energy within the company. When the team has positive energy, things just start to happen. That energy is felt all around, and it's what turns a mediocre new project or initiative into a successful one.

When you are in an optimistic mood, your brain sees things from a successful perspective. You make new connections and you bring different worlds together—that is what innovation is all about.

continued

Ask venture capital investors what they look for in new companies, and they will tell you that the energy of the team is paramount.

Compare that with a team that is not excited. Employees' focus becomes about getting the job done and going home. There is no spark. Boring, stagnant energy will not foster connections, and even the most promising projects will die. Plus, it's no fun!

MY FIRST INTERN

Being burned-out does not foster creative problem solving. If your mind is full of to-do items, how can there be space for new ideas? Now that I was stress-free, however, I could bring back creativity to the business process. Expanding a business requires new systems that will make everything run well. And developing these new systems requires creativity and energy.

Internet marketing was a big reason for the success of DVD Your Memories. I realized in 2009 that it would make sense to put more focus on that area. I decided to create a part-time internship for someone to help me with search engine marketing.

Normally I don't like internships, because if a job is low paid or unpaid, there is less incentive for interns to show up on time and do their best work. Additionally, it takes a lot of time and energy to manage interns, as they are expecting to learn from you. In this case, however, hiring an intern made sense. Although the offer was for an unpaid role, the intern would likely earn a full- or part-time position if he or she did well.

After receiving a flood of applications for this internship and interviewing a few prospects, I was not impressed. Mostly I was getting marketing types—talkative personalities with questionable computer skills. I gave them the computer skills tests, and none could compare to many of our current technicians. Whoever got hired for this position would be working side by side with me and needed to be able to keep up.

Then it hit me. Maybe Chris, who was recently hired as a part-time videotape transfer technician, was the right person. He was tech savvy, easy to get along with, and a hard worker. He always showed up on time, and he went above and beyond his job description when we needed him. Chris did not have a background in internet marketing, but I assured him that he would be trained. All he needed to do was work hard and absorb what I would be teaching him, and the full-time position was his for the taking.

Chris accepted the internship role in addition to his current role as a part-time technician and worked alongside me every day. We learned together, and within a month or two Chris became my right-hand man. Within six months, he was more knowledgeable than I was when it came to internet marketing.

His writing skills were excellent as well, so he could edit our website and write blog posts. Chris not only became our full-time internet marketing guy, but was instrumental in the company's growth because so much of it hinged on our search marketing.

It just goes to show how someone can work hard, get recognized, jump on an opportunity, and—within a relatively short amount of time—find themselves with a salary, benefits, and eventually enough money to support a family. As a business owner, providing these types of opportunities for personal and professional growth is what I am most proud of.

Tip: Learn to Delegate

Part of growing a company is learning to delegate tasks and responsibilities to others. There is only so much one person can

continued

do by themselves. Here are the three rules I always follow when delegating:

1. Choose superstars only. Basically, only delegate to someone you know can get the job done.

2. Give clear instructions and deadlines. If you leave any ambiguity in your instructions, then expect the unexpected. And you *must set a deadline, or you might be waiting forever.*

3. Check back. Make a note to check back if you don't hear anything on the deadline date. And check back again when the job is complete. Make sure to praise a job well done or train on how to improve—and ask for feedback.

If something delegated did not go according to plan, it was always because I forgot one of these rules (usually the one about giving precise instructions)!

WHAT NEXT?

DVD Your Memories was going full steam ahead. I moved back to San Diego and found that my old life wasn't working for me anymore. I needed to get out of a relationship and work on some personal goals. Despite the growth of the company, I began to feel a bit out of balance and generally not happy.

My breakup was a long, drawn-out process that left me feeling drained. Between the work of growing a business and my relationship ending, I needed a breather. I decided to go back to Thailand—to the same place I went before starting the business and again before opening the OC store. But this time would be different: I would be going alone, and I did not purchase a return ticket. In fact, I planned nothing—not even a hotel room on the day I arrived.

It ended up being just the kind of interlude I needed.

AN INTERLUDE FOR PERSONAL GROWTH

I needed to grow. One of the challenges that awaited me back at home was being able to meet new people and make friends on my own. My social anxiety made it a challenge to introduce myself to new people and forge connections. I was pretty good at doing this in a structured environment at work, but those people were essentially paid to get along with me. Developing a business meant getting outside the office, asserting myself to meet new people and construct partnerships. I felt the need to challenge myself in an unstructured environment where I would be forced to make friends—and see how I could get along.

I arrived in Bangkok with just a backpack and took a taxi to the only place I knew: Khao San Road, the same place featured in the movie *The Beach* with Leonardo DiCaprio, in the scene where his friend dies in the hostel. The street is a bouillabaisse of bars, strip clubs, massage parlors, restaurants, and travel agencies. But walking the actual pavement is where the action is.

My first week was spent drinking in the middle of the street until my thoughts were blurred and my emotions were almost completely numbed. Sometimes I would walk to the bars and play pool with the "bar girls" for drinks. Even when drunk, I would usually beat them. My goal was to make friends, but I still couldn't put myself out there. I wandered the streets a loner.

After being on Khao San Road for more than a week, I decided to head north, to Chiang Mai—a place I had not been to. I stayed at Julie's Guesthouse for less than a dollar a day. One day I booked a downhill bike ride from a mountain monastery to the river at the bottom. A half hour into the ride, the weather changed, and it began to downpour. Everyone fell, even the guides. One guy lost a lot of skin off his back after he completely flipped over. Eventually we made it and took a much-needed cleansing swim in the river.

Later that week I met a group of four fun and crazy Australian guys. We all went to dinner one night. All five of us piled into a two-seat *tuk-tuk* (three-wheeled taxi). I was sitting on the battery next to the driver; two of the other guys were sitting in back, and two were hanging off the back. After dinner and plenty of drinks, we decided to hit up a Muay Thai fight.

After more drinks, we had the grand idea to challenge some of the Thai boxers in the ring. The Australians were much bigger and did well, but I'm sure the Thai boxers were taking it easy on them. Reluctantly, I went last.

My opponent was a couple inches shorter than me but much stockier. The first round was even. For the second round, my "corner" told me to turn it up a notch. I found success with punching, and then when my opponent punched back, I would tie up his arms so he couldn't land anything significant.

I'm not sure at what point my strategy failed, but after missing my punch, my opponent landed a clean one. I staggered back, dazed. After shaking it off for a few seconds, I came back for more. I was not able to stand up straight, and he clocked me with another one. I grabbed at the air trying to tie him up once again, but it was no use. Another sweeping punch landed flush on my left eye. I spun around and landed on my ass.

After making it back to my feet, I was not interested in any more exchanges with him. The bell rang at last, marking the end of the second round and the fight. It was called a draw, and we both got our hands raised, smiling. Later, I made friends with the Thai fighter, and we collected money from the crowd together.

The next day I realized how bad my black eye was, and I must have twisted my ankle at some point during the fight, because walking was painful. But this type of adventure was just what I needed.

It is a funny thing, getting into a fight. It actually has an extremely calming effect; those things that normally caused me anxiety didn't seem to matter much anymore. I gained perspective on what is worth being afraid of. After this experience, it became much easier to get over my anxiety and make friends.

After Chiang Mai, I traveled to the Phi Phi Islands, a place I had been to before and quite enjoyed for its relaxing atmosphere. On the minibus from the airport, I met Sam and Nino—the first of many friends I'd made since forcing myself out of my comfort zone while traveling.

From Phi Phi, I caught a boat to Railay and did some rock climbing. I met an Israeli couple on the bus while playing cards, then eventually made my way to Ko Pha-Ngan, one of my favorite places in the world.

I knew to go to Cookies Bungalow, a place I had stayed previously out on the north side of the island—far away from Haad Rin, where the famous full-moon party happens each month. At Cookies, I met and made friends with the owner of a bar when we battled at billiards. As the full-moon party got closer, the friends I had made in the other cities in Thailand all came to the island.

Each reacquainting reminded me that I had accomplished my goal—I had learned to get over my social anxiety and make friends. And now the benefits of making these friends were realized once again, as we all partied together under the full moon on the beach in Thailand.

Tip: Plan the Right Type of Break

Taking extreme breaks became a pattern for me during the growth of DVD Your Memories. Extreme breaks are needed when you work extremely hard. The brain is like a muscle, and you can't just work it incessantly and never give it a rest.

My obsession with the business had to be in direct proportion to the amount of "break" in my break. If I was somewhat relaxed and not overworking myself, then a break might just be for a three-day weekend. But if I was completely burned out, then my break needed to be complete: no phone, no internet, no way to connect . . . a real, complete break, long enough for two to three days of business-brain withdrawal so I could find a new mental equilibrium, and then spend time luxuriating in a nonbusiness state!

I can't stress how important this is. Just remember: more burnout/stress = more extreme break. It is the only way.

READY FOR THE NEXT STEP

The Thailand trip with no return ticket was a major turning point in my professional and personal story. Looking back, this moment in time is symbolic for many reasons.

It started out as a repeat of the original trip I made during my final college spring break, which was made possible by money from making DVDs for Daniel. That first trip had led me to realize that I was successful in returning to my computer nerd roots, to what I loved. So Thailand became a place of transformation and learning for me.

This time, I went to learn about making better personal connections, something I knew I needed and couldn't get at home in familiar surroundings. I knew my Thailand trip was done about a month and a half after I arrived, because I had accomplished what I'd set out to do. I'd grown as a person and acquired a skill that would be instrumental in my development as a leader and as a well-rounded person.

I'd also had enough time to rediscover inspiration about DVD Your Memories. Two stores both working well, improved personal skills, and a renewed energy for making DVD Your Memories stronger than ever—that's how the business and I were positioned as the summer of 2009 turned into fall. I was ready to get back to work.

I didn't know exactly what the future would hold or what direction I would go, but I felt prepared to take on anything.

Online Resources:
Executive Management Coaching

Visit startuptosold.com for up-to-date resources on the following topics.

- Personal productivity tools and methods

- Understanding micromanagement vs. undermanagement

- How to delegate

- My favorite management books

PART II

TO SOLD

CHAPTER 13

PREPARING FOR ACT II

When I got back from my six-week hiatus in Thailand, one of the first things I decided to do was purchase a new car. To this day, I always feel nervous when purchasing something for myself. It probably comes from being short on money growing up. But I had managed to pay off my student loan balance, which was a huge deal for me because I was very uncomfortable with debt. Now that I was out of debt, I could spend a little more money.

It was time to reward myself.

REWARDING HARD WORK

I had been driving a twelve-year-old Chevy Cavalier that my dad gave to me when I was a sophomore in college. I used that car for everything: carrying surfboards to the ocean, going to work at the electronics store, dragging multiple tables and giant televisions to the farmers markets. The car had served me well, and I felt a personal attachment to it. But it was getting older and showing signs of wear. Life changes, and it makes sense to upgrade your life when the time is right.

I bought a new car for three reasons. First, I needed to reward myself for working hard. Working hard feels good in and of itself, but it helps the reward systems in your brain to have something tangible that you see every day. I hadn't bought anything else of value for myself yet, save the long trip to Thailand, so this was the material object I needed.

Second, spending money changes the brain a little bit. Making this purchase helped my brain realize that I had moved up a level. There was a new baseline level of success and income that I now assumed was normal. Now my brain would work somewhat differently to maintain this new normal.

Third, I needed to look the part. As a business owner, I thought I should drive a car that echoed who I am and represented the company. I wanted to drive something that was respectable.

I ended up purchasing a 2006 Acura RSX. It got great gas mileage (about 30 mpg) for those constant trips up and down from San Diego to Orange County. And best of all, with manual transmission, it was fun to drive.

Unfortunately, not everything was rosy in my world, and I needed to access the positive energy I'd regained by traveling. The Orange County store was struggling quite a bit. A week before I got back from Thailand, our full-time image scanning technician (one of the best employees at the store) had to be let go, which meant Richard needed to hire and train in the only department that he was not yet knowledgeable enough to train for.

Then another really good employee put in his two weeks' notice, leaving Richard the lone survivor in the OC location. It takes at least a couple weeks to hire a new technician and another two weeks to complete basic training. It was already mid-October, and our holiday rush season was around the corner, so the OC store became a super-high priority.

With these issues, plus Richard watching over the highest-value project we had ever acquired, the City of Irvine order, it became necessary for me to go back to Orange County and work on the store. I ended up renting a room there for the remainder of the year to make sure the OC office survived.

THE EARLY DAYS OF REMOTE COMMUNICATION

Nowadays, communicating with people who aren't physically in the same place is no big deal. But back in 2009, it was a real challenge. Until the OC store opened, all of DVD Your Memories was located under the same roof. Everyone worked together and could communicate freely. Now, with me out of San Diego for the better half of 2009, the mode of communication had to change.

Email has been the communication method of choice for distributed teams since the advent of the internet, and has remained largely unchanged since that time. I like email for certain one-on-one communications. It can be archived and easily searched, and there is value in taking your time to respond thoughtfully. However, there are many other circumstances where email simply falls short.

For quick, short communications, email is too slow. In those cases, we started using Google Chat (Gchat), an instant messaging application built alongside Gmail. Gchat is helpful because of the green dot that signifies someone is available to chat—akin to someone's office door being open. Knowing someone is available makes it easy to get answers immediately and move projects along quickly. And if people want to be left alone, they can change their status to signify this, just as someone would close their office door.

Most days I would have three to five Gchat windows open simultaneously, enabling me to have three to five "meetings" at once, with no one overhearing anyone else or getting confused. Each meeting was self-contained. I could work on internet marketing with Keith, talk to Bryan about the San Diego store, and work with Brandi on marketing and financials—all at the same time.

Email faces its biggest limitation when it comes to group messaging and collaboration. You know what happens when you get three or more people in an email chain, each person using the Reply All button: the email chain can quickly become hundreds of lines long. Finding a link or a small piece of information someone posted a week ago becomes an insufferable task. *Which email was it in? How far down should I scroll? What's with all these brackets? Okay, I give up!* Email is not the right tool for group communication.

The other tool we started to employ was Google Wave (which became Apache Wave a year later and ultimately was discontinued in 2018). Google Wave was like Google Docs in that you could create a document and edit it simultaneously; each person could see what others were typing in real time. Also, Wave had a function that was much like a forum, where you could respond to someone else in-line. You could "mention" others so that they would be notified about something. And it had a great system of alerting you if a Wave had been updated.

There were a lot of gadgets that could be added to a Wave that allowed for polls, maps, and many other useful items. And you could see who wrote what, as well as replay the history of a Wave so there would be full accountability.

We would make a Wave for each project. Then we would outline the project on the Wave, in text form, and magically, the steps would be ironed out via a quick dialogue. Questions would be brought up and could be answered by anyone on that Wave. It was like a superhuman form of intelligence. Even an in-person meeting was not this effective or efficient, as each person on a Wave had the combined knowledge of the entire internet as well as their own networks. In our company, Google Wave became more popular than email for getting things done.

Google Wave has been discontinued for quite some time now, but today there are plenty of other ways to collaborate with people at a distance. A certain technology might work best for your industry or company—something that any business owner will discover with a little trial and error, especially as they grow beyond a single location.

> ### Tip: Take Advantage of Communication Technologies
>
> At the time of printing this book, I would recommend Notion.so as the best team collaboration web-based software.

ACCOUNTING FOR TWO LOCATIONS

When you only have one store, the books are easy. Everything can fit in one column. The overhead (staff) can be combined with the single store because it is all the same. But when you have multiple locations, you need to have a little more finesse to keep things in order. I needed to find a new accounting system.

Brandi and I decided that we would use the class function within QuickBooks to separate each store into its own class, and we created a new class for "overhead" and another for "growth." The class function allows you to look at each class separately rather than combining everything; on a P&L report, for example, there is one column for each class. Our spreadsheet told us how much the OC store was making versus the San Diego store.

	CLASS 1 Orange County	CLASS 2 San Diego	TOTAL
Ordinary Income/Expense			
Income			
Fees	1,000.00	2,000.00	3,000.00
Product Sales	2,000.00	4,000.00	6,000.00
Services	30,000.00	60,000.00	90,000.00
Total Income	33,000.00	66,000.00	99,000.00
Cost of Goods Sold			
Cost of Goods Sold	3,000.00	6,000.00	9,000.00
Total COGS	3,000.00	6,000.00	9,000.00
Gross Profit	30,000.00	60,000.00	90,000.00
Expense			
Computers and IT			
Computer Software	5.00	5.00	10.00
Computers and IT: Other	200.00	600.00	800.00
Total Computers and IT	205.00	605.00	810.00
Advertising	5,000.00	7,000.00	12,000.00
Automobile Expense	100.00	120.00	220.00
Bank Service Charges			
Merchant Credit Card Fees	1,000.00	2,000.00	3,000.00
Bank Service Charges: Other	10.00	40.00	50.00
Total Bank Service Charges	1,010.00	2,040.00	3,050.00

Figure 14: Structure of the multistore accounting spreadsheet.

Our overhead class was pretty much just the salaries of Brandi, Keith, and me plus any other expenses related to this effort. Now we could see what each store would make with and without the overhead. And when it came to profit sharing, we would divide the overhead cost by the number of stores. That way if we opened more stores, theoretically, the amount of overhead per store would decrease.

But what about the expenses that I could write off personally? If I wanted to buy a new phone or laptop, host business meetings with friends, or attend conferences, I had an opportunity to write them off. These things were not necessary for the operation of the current stores, however, and I felt like they should not be categorized as overhead and thereby affect the bonus amounts for the store managers. Still, they were considered a write-off expense as far as taxes were concerned. How should the accounting system handle these?

The answer is the growth class. This fourth class was for expenses related to my efforts at growth that I thought were unfair to deduct from the profit-sharing system. Now I could see at a glance the amount I was spending versus overhead, and versus each store.

It was a phenomenal system because it was so easy. Store managers had access to the books, so it was transparent to everyone what was going on. I told the managers about the plan and trained them on it. My other reason for implementing the growth class was so everyone knew that fairness was always top of mind for me. Richard and Bryan had to know that I was always going to look out for them. And if they had any doubts, they could see all the transactions for themselves.

Between QuickBooks, Wave, Gchat, and other technologies, we were constantly innovating and creating new tools to solve any issues that came up. Unfortunately, technology can only solve so much. When you're dealing with the government, you need to reach a little deeper into your bag of tools.

IN TROUBLE WITH THE IRS

The beginning of 2010 was a time of rest, or at least nongrowth. We took advantage of this calm period to research new marketing and sales opportunities in our local area. We thought in more detail about our customers—what they would be interested in and where we could find them.

I had the idea of reaching out to the scrapbooking community after seeing that my mom and sister were into this crafting-with-photos hobby. So we rented a booth at the 2010 Scrapbook Expo at the Orange County Fairgrounds in Southern California. The weekend fair went well for us. The success of the customer research was overshadowed, however, by an unexpected interaction at the booth that led to the realization we'd been making a major error in our business operations.

A woman with a clipboard approached our display, and we began chatting pleasantly about the business. She asked a lot of questions, more than most consumers usually would, and I answered them truthfully, disclosing details about how we charged customers for our products and services. Whether it was due to my naivete at that time or her experience discreetly interviewing small business owners at trade shows like this, I truly didn't get any sense that I could be putting my business at risk by answering her questions. After she told me that she was from the agency that collects tax on the sales of goods and services in California, I took a step back and realized what had happened.

I explained to her that we had not been charging sales tax to our customers because our work transferring old media to digital format was considered a service, and therefore was not subject to sales tax. We weren't selling a physical product, so there was no reason to collect from the consumer.

Turns out we were wrong.

Our policies were always the most favorable toward the customers, but this time we had gone too far. On impulse, I considered telling this government employee that if I needed to pay back taxes and penalties, it would make my business bankrupt and then we wouldn't be paying any other sales tax in the future! We ended our conversation with her handing me her business card and letting me know that she would be contacting us for an audit.

Once I returned to the office on Monday, I talked with Brandi about the situation. We were unsure about the damage done by not having understood how sales tax regulations applied to the unique line of business we were in. So we decided to take the approach of being completely, undeniably, and almost obnoxiously transparent, factual, and cooperative!

Brandi spent the next few months corresponding with the agency: calling the representative weekly to check in, leaving detailed messages, faxing, emailing, and generally being all about every letter of the law. We also sent in evidence that companies in our industry, and in similar industries, had also not been charging sales tax.

The effort and attention to the audit paid off. In the end, we were not penalized for the mistake. We just received written direction about how to correctly charge sales tax to customers for the services we offered.

There is a greater lesson to be learned from the story of the lady with the clipboard—not just about how to deal with the government, but about the mindset of an entrepreneur. This is about risk versus reward and why I don't avoid making these types of mistakes.

Every action you take in business comes with potential risk. Some examples include the following:

ACTION	RISK	REWARD
Hire employee	They turn out to be terrible and set your company back months	You are able to grow your business
Advertising in a magazine	Lose money	Make profit; Gain new customers and connections
Optimize an operational process	Screw up and the quality of your product goes down	Do a good job and quality or speed improves
Promote business to potential customers	They are a government employee trying to catch you doing something wrong	You find a new customer

But to grow a business, you have to take action—that's a given. And since every action has a potential risk, you also have to take risks. I'm not a risk-taker—in fact, I'm very risk averse. Contrary to popular belief, so are many other entrepreneurs. But risk is almost always outweighed by reward for taking an action when you add in the second part of that reward: learning from your mistakes.

Each time your action leads to a mistake or a reward, you learn something. And it just so happens that you learn much more from your mistakes than from your rewards. So even when you fail at something, there is a massive benefit from learning. So now, for every action you undertake as an entrepreneur, you have two possible outcomes:

1. You succeed and learn.

2. You fail and learn even more.

The more mistakes you make, the more you learn and the more savvy you become as an entrepreneur. And as if this weren't enough, remember that mistakes are scaled with the size of your business. That means it's best to make your mistakes early! And guess what: as long as you are growing your business, it's always early.

At most companies, mistakes are hidden or avoided altogether. At DVD Your Memories, we had a culture of being loud and proud about our mistakes. The team realized that the number of mistakes we made were directly proportional to the success we would experience. And it had to start with me. Remember, this type of culture has to come from the top down. That's the only way to build an environment where everyone feels comfortable enough to try new things, fail, learn, and try again.

CREATING A TRIBE OF NERDS

The lull at the beginning of 2010 also allowed us to become more acquainted with the media transfer industry in an online fashion. Since we were all nerds, it was easy for us to start posting in forums, and we even started our own blog. Previously, we would be the ones asking questions on other forums, but now we were answering other people's questions.

I didn't know it at the time, but we were starting to follow the methodology outlined in a great book by Seth Godin, called *Tribes*. A tribe is a group of people who share a similar interest and can talk about it at length, learning from each other. They know the same authors, speakers, and other "tribal leaders." Seth Godin says that you need to become a tribe leader, and his book outlines a variety of ways to do that.

At DVD Your Memories we were exercising one of those methods: becoming a knowledge leader within our tribe of media transfer. Between writing posts on forums and technical posts on our own blog, we slowly became the experts whom others could trust. As we curated interesting and relevant topics, our blog incrementally started to get more popular. One of the more famous posts was a video guide on how to perform a tape repair.

A tape repair was needed when your VCR had rewound your videocassette tape so fast that it snapped the tape in two. This was a nightmare if you didn't know what you were doing. Fortunately, we had been fulfilling orders for tape repair for years and had perfected it. Chris, our internet marketing guy, started writing guides on a variety of subjects like this. Many of them even helped people transfer their own media so they wouldn't need us at all.

Media transfer is not hard for most types of media. Scanning photos and copying videotapes to DVD doesn't take too much technical expertise or money. We would say that it was akin to painting your house: It is not difficult, but it does take time. And that is why there are painting companies. For a house, however, if you do something wrong, I suppose you can just paint over it, or replace your carpets if you spill a can of paint. But when you are transferring media—something that cannot be replaced—and you screw it up, many times you can't recover from your mistake. Especially if you throw away the original media.

Our strategy was to help those people who were trying to do things themselves. This would create value for them, but not for us . . . at least not initially. But let me ask you this: if you were not technically inclined but you wanted your analog media preserved, who would you go to for advice? Probably the nerdiest person you know. That person would then either recommend something for you or refer you to a company that knows what it is doing. We wanted to be that company.

Becoming a knowledge leader within our tribe made good business sense. We wanted the nerds to be impressed enough to trust us, and then recommend us to their friends. And guess what: they did!

Lesson Learned: Throw Your Weight Around When You Grow Big Enough

One of the things we realized during these relatively peaceful months of 2010 was that we were finally big enough to start throwing around our weight a little more. That's a real milestone when you're growing a business!

For example, we realized that we were purchasing double the amount of materials that we used to purchase, including everything from blank DVDs, ink, and computers to software and other office supplies. That meant we could now pressure suppliers to give us discounts. In economics, they refer to this as "economies of scale."

We took this opportunity to talk to our suppliers and inquire about any bulk discounts. Lo and behold, it was easy to negotiate savings on many items. For most of the items, we didn't even have to negotiate at all. We simply asked about lower prices because we were buying so much more now. Most vendors were happy to let us in on their bulk pricing so they could keep us as customers. A win-win!

THE 2ND SECOND STORE

A few months into 2010, we noticed that the OC store continued to underperform regarding day-to-day sales. It had already paid off our initial investment, but the store wasn't making as much as it should in such a wealthy part of the country. After a few meetings, we started to get a hunch as to why.

The OC store was located a couple blocks from the Pacific Ocean. One factor in choosing the office was that we had a partial ocean view (if you were on the second story and jumped high enough). But there was a huge downside of being so close to the ocean: driving distances. All else being equal, we knew people would be more likely to "pop in" and visit a business that was closer to them. Those who lived close to the ocean were great customers for us, but those who lived inland would be less likely to drive the extra distance to our store.

The realization came from looking at how many people lived within a ten-mile radius of the store. Looking at the map below, you can see that much of our typical driving radius was covering the ocean. The problem was, only one customer ever popped in from the ocean. Fish were not placing many orders with us.

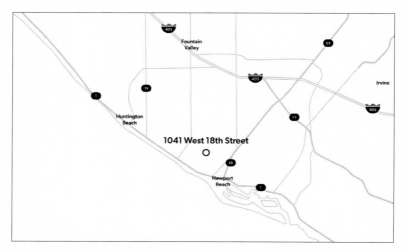

Figure 15: Noncentral location of our 1st second store in Orange County.

Our business model was to have one local store that would serve an entire county, and we realized that being centrally located within a county was important. The San Diego store had always been in Kearny Mesa, a subdivision of San Diego that was centrally located in terms of the population of San Diego County and located at the intersection of five freeways. And we had experienced success there.

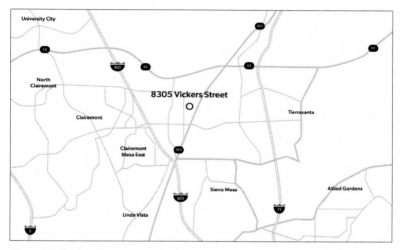

Figure 16: The San Diego store in Kearny Mesa—easy to reach by much of the population of San Diego County.

So we decided to apply the same criteria—central in terms of population, and easy access enabled by multiple highways—to pick a better location for the OC store. Ultimately we decided to move to Irvine, the city for which we had completed that large job in 2009. Though only about six miles inland from Costa Mesa, Irvine is centrally located and the center point of most freeways in Orange County.

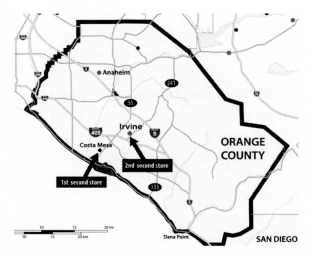

Figure 17: Location of the 2nd second store.

We had a one-year lease on the property in Orange County, so as our lease expired, we left the area and moved into a nice office in a business park in Irvine. We still had the frugal mindset and moved everything ourselves with a U-Haul. Bryan took the beer out of the ceiling and put it into the ceiling of the new office in Irvine.

It turned out that we had made the right move. Within a month, our sales nearly doubled! Richard's store was now doing just as much revenue as Bryan's, and both were extremely profitable. I was overjoyed and had just learned a very important lesson: location matters!

TURNING A CORNER

The end of 2009 and the beginning of 2010 turned out to be a rewarding period for the business. We got the OC store up to speed. Google Wave kept the two stores in touch and in sync.

Richard hired the new employees and trained them. He had taken a risk by moving to and heading up the OC store on the faith that DVD Your Memories was going to do well by him. He had a rough go of it with HR issues, but we saw them through.

Meanwhile, Bryan was holding down the San Diego store without me there. Brandi had handled all the new store-opening tasks and onboarding new employees on top of her regular tasks.

The hard work paid off. December 2009 had been our most profitable month as a company to date. It was San Diego's best December ever, it was the OC store's best month ever, and now we anticipated a far more profitable future at our new OC location. The City of Irvine project was complete, and we received the final payment. Everyone pulled together, and we had one of the best and by far most profitable years in our short history.

Now we could focus on how to continue our sales growth.

Online Resources: Next-Level Systems, Advanced Marketing, & Building Sustainable Advantages

Visit startuptosold.com for up-to-date resources on the following topics.

- Remote management tools

- Team collaboration software

- Recommended accounting resources

- How to become a tribe leader

- Advanced social media marketing strategies

CHAPTER 14

DIAGNOSING AND SOLVING SALES CHALLENGES

Making a bold decision—like moving an entire store—is a larger task than a few pages in a book can describe. It feels good to make big moves and have them pay off. It instills confidence that you can do the right thing. And everyone gets to share in the success.

Even though sales improved after we made the move to our new location, we all recognized there was still work to do around sales. The problem we recognized was that 80% of our sales were coming in from just one source, Google AdWords. Google's massive influence on our business was risky, because if something happened to this one source of inbound sales, 80% of our revenue would be gone overnight.

As a company, we were getting better and better at our operational capabilities, and we were confident there was no other company that could perform transfers as well as us. This makes sense because at our core, we were computer nerds who focused on technical proficiency. Unfortunately, this created an imbalance in our company, skewing heavily toward operations rather than sales, and I knew that.

I couldn't imagine that Google AdWords was the only profitable method to gain new customers. This is why I had tried the Scrapbook Expo, and now I jumped at another opportunity: a live television appearance.

My television debut was on *San Diego Living*, a local television morning show that had contacted us about being on a live, in-studio segment. Of course, this was exciting and totally unexpected. We didn't think anyone paid attention to our little company. I remember thinking what a great opportunity this was: We would be seen by thousands of local residents. It would make for a fantastic video clip that we could put on our website. And it was just a fun thing to show off to my friends and family. But there was one big problem: I was deathly afraid of being in front of an audience.

The last time I had to talk in front of a large group of people was in a psychology class in college. Now I had this TV appearance. They wouldn't tell me in advance what the questions were going to be, but I figured they would be about media transfer. This upcoming event dominated my mind. I needed to figure out this whole social anxiety thing.

At the time, I was listening to Tony Robbins's CDs, and he had a technique that I thought might work. If you wanted to change something about your life or rewire your brain in some way, he advised using a mantra. One stipulation was that the wording had to state the positive. For instance, my mantra couldn't be *I'm not scared in social situations*, because that was a negative mantra. I thought about this for a while and came up with *I'm calm, cool, and collected under pressure*. That became my mantra.

For almost two weeks, I said the mantra to myself, usually silently. When I was driving, eating, going to sleep, taking a shower in the morning, working out at the gym—anytime I had a free moment, I said, "I'm calm, cool, and collected under pressure." At the end of the two weeks, I didn't feel as anxious when thinking about appearing on the TV show.

Brandi knew about my social anxiety, so we decided that the two of us would go on the show together. The day finally arrived, and I was still saying my mantra in the green room until finally we were up. Brandi and I appeared on the show and did an excellent job. The host even threw a curveball into her questioning, and I did an okay job at processing and responding. The whole time I reminded myself, *I'm calm under pressure.* And I was.

I wish I could report that being featured on a local television show brought in a bunch of new clients, but all we received was a few orders from viewers of the show.

In business, there are so many paths to take, and you have to go down a lot of wrong paths to find out where they lead. That is a necessary part of learning to be a savvy business owner. I'm proud of these "mistakes."

At this point, everything I'd tried to diversify our revenue had proven futile: the Scrapbook Expo, the TV show, magazines, local newspapers, postcards, and other things alike. I was still going to the farmers market, and that brought in some steady business. But we had yet to crack the code when it came to diversifying our revenue from Google.

My intention was still to "level up" the sales efforts of the company, so if I couldn't make a breakthrough using traditional sales channels such as TV, print, and so forth, I would move down the path of revenue and optimize what we could control—everything from responding to a phone or email inquiry all the way through to the final sale. And one question always stumped me: a strange pattern of recurring drops in our sales.

> **Tip:** Face Your Fears
>
> Though my TV debut didn't bring in a lot of customers, I still welcomed the experience to face my fears. It was another stepping-stone in my journey from job hustler to successful entrepreneur. Many, many times I had to step out of my comfort zone and take on a challenge that scared me.
>
> The appearance on *San Diego Living* was a continuation of the challenge I'd posed to myself on my most recent trip to Thailand: refusing to live in fear of social anxiety. Building a successful business means constantly stretching self-imposed limitations and redefining your comfort zone.

DIAGNOSING SALES DROPS

Another thing that always caused me a lot of anxiety, because I didn't understand why it happened, was when sales would slip at one of the stores.

We had a long sales cycle. Customers would first look up some type of scanning question online. Then they would find our website. They most likely would call our local store and speak with one of our technicians. Then, we hoped, they would make an appointment or just come in. They would have their order taken by one of the technicians. A week or so later, the order would be finished, and we would call them to come pick it up. They would come in and pick it up, and we would call to thank them a week or so later. That was it.

With all those variables, how could we tease out why our sales might be slipping so that we could fix it quicker the next time it happened?

We all knew about diagnosing computers. The way to fix a problem with a computer is to narrow down the problem. If a computer is not recognizing your USB thumb drive, for example, you put that same drive into another computer to see if there is something wrong with the drive itself or the port. What if we used the same methodology to diagnose our sales?

We decided to implement a phone and sales graph to log our phone calls. Whenever a store got a sales call, the tech answering the phone would record it on the tally for that day. It only took a few seconds, but the information it relayed was worth a ton.

Now, if sales were down for one month and phone calls were also down, we knew the problem lay somewhere before the phone call (such as the website or the internet marketing). If the number of phone calls was normal but fewer customers were coming, we knew the problem could be with how the phone calls were handled. And this led us to another discovery.

Sometimes after a store had a busy couple of weeks, its sales would suddenly drop off. And this was not due to a lack of online clicks or phone calls. It was something else. Eventually, just to see what would happen, I decided to "plug the USB port into a different computer"—that is to say, I routed our phone calls from a busy store (USB port) to a less busy store (another computer).

Almost overnight, sales shot up! The new protocol worked. If we had too many calls going to a store that was busy processing orders, that led to fewer sales. We adjusted and saw the impact almost immediately.

We learned a great lesson from this, and we named it "throttling": it is what happens when you have the same employees answering customer calls *and* doing the work. When those employees feel busy, they will self-adjust their own workload in the ways they can control. And sometimes those ways can be subtle.

I believe customers can feel the energy of a store when they call. They can tell whether the store wants their business or not. Feeling like a company wants their business is the prime factor that will cause a customer to come in. If customers don't feel this because the person answering the phone is less than enthusiastic or sounds distracted, they won't come in.

Because this type of energy transfer is so subtle, it's almost impossible to train. When there is momentum in a store, the employees are feeling good, not overstressed, and happy about their jobs, and the customers will feel it and want to come in. But if the employees feel overworked, their voices will convey this energy on the phone; the customers will feel it and will not come in. Now that we knew about throttling, we took steps to avoid it. We used the new protocol for directing calls to the less-busy store, or having the store manager take as many calls as possible to lighten the load for the busy technicians.

Now that we knew who were the right people to answer the incoming phone calls, we optimized how those phone calls went.

IMPROVING OUR PHONE SALES TECHNIQUES

I told our technicians to expect some secret shopper phone calls coming in. I suppose it was not so secret after all, because I told them ahead of time. But I also made sure they knew the secret shopper results would be made available to them—and would not affect anyone's raise in pay.

I knew if I were in the technicians' shoes, I would be apprehensive about the whole process. So one of the most important things was to keep this process as positive as I could. It was simply a chance to learn about how they might be more effective with customers on the phone.

I paid my older sister to call the stores, follow a script, and write down the key points. She tallied different elements: Did our technicians mention one competitive advantage? Did they ask for the appointment? Did they sound confident? How many times did they say "um" during the conversation? These were some of the things we needed to know.

The secret shopper exercise let everyone know that they were responsible for implementing the simple sales skills they were taught, by hitting all these important points during a phone call. Some technicians were already great, and others needed some work. One funny result was that Bryan won the award for the highest number of "ums"! Goes to show you that everyone can work on something.

UPSELLING

Now that we were on a roll and getting a handle on improving our sales strategy, I shifted my attention one more step down the sales cycle, to upselling: when a customer comes in thinking about getting one level of service, and the salesperson convinces them to go with a higher level of service or to purchase an add-on product.

You see this happen every time you go to a restaurant and they offer you dessert at the end of the meal. It also happens at most electronic stores when they offer you a warranty or add-on accessories. Most of the media transfers we sold had either different levels of service or an add-on product that the customer could purchase. For example, slides could be scanned at either 2000, 3000, or 4000 dpi (dots per inch). The higher the dpi, the better the digital representation would be. And of course, it took more time to scan at higher resolutions, and therefore the cost was higher.

As a company, if we increased the upsell and add-on percentage for each sale, we would increase our profits considerably. But what was the right way to train our technicians to work on upselling?

Back at the electronics store, I had been given the upsell numbers nearly every hour. The sales manager would come around with not only the percentage, but our rank within the company for the day, the month, and the quarter. It was very cool, and I remember being somewhat motivated to help make our store the best.

Today we refer to this technique as "gamifying" sales. Providing a competitive environment not only is an example of gamifying, however, but also plays into the Hawthorne effect, which states that employees will improve in areas in which they know they are being measured.

Brandi and I created a spreadsheet that would be shared throughout the company. It was color coded and included all the major upsells and add-ons. It had dpi increases, premium versus competitive film transfer, email mailing list signups, and a few other important measures. At the end of each month, Brandi would send the raw reports to Chris, who would input the final numbers in the spreadsheet. Now we could not only see which store had the highest percentage of upsells, but also drill down to individual employee efforts.

Again, it was important to make the experience as positive as possible. Some employees were great technicians and not the best salespeople, and we were asking them to do both. There were no penalties for not doing well—but there were incentives for improving.

Lesson Learned: Skills Development Offers Great Leverage

Improving your employees' sales skills provides great leverage no matter whether you have one store or two (or even more). For example, when we implemented a new sales technique that increased the upsell percentage of slide scanning, the impact wasn't multiplied just by the five employees at one store, but almost instantly by the ten people we had working at both of our stores. The same amount of work on my part (as the sales manager) to identify improvement was paying greater dividends than ever before.

WEAVING A SALES MENTALITY INTO OUR CULTURE

Over time, each measure we put on that color-coded spreadsheet improved. I'm not talking about a few percentage points here and there; I'm talking about more than doubling the percentages. This made a huge impact on our total revenue and our bottom line.

There was a side benefit to all this tracking: sales techniques started to be part of the daily conversation at stores, as it was for Yiga and me way back at the big-box electronics store. For example, someone would come up with a phrase that significantly increased the number of customers signing up for our email newsletter. The employees in that store would all switch to using the same technique in order to improve sales metrics. As an incentive, they'd receive something like free Jamba Juice.

I started to ask each store manager what their staff was doing differently that led to better results, and then I would enlist that store to help refine the sales training for everyone. We were creating our own best practices by making incremental gains in each sales area.

Once again, a lot of our improvements came down to expressing appreciation for our employees' hard work. Sharing praise for individual excellence allowed me to continue the emphasis on sales and selling skills throughout the company. As our sales continued to improve, I started sending emails to the employees who either had the highest number of upsells in an area or had improved their score significantly. A simple and short email, maybe just a couple of sentences, was enough to offer my sincere thanks. Most of the time I got a reply that was also very positive.

Everyone felt good about what we were doing in the company, and it showed.

Online Resources: Optimizing Sales

Visit startuptosold.com for up-to-date resources on the following topics.

- Diagnosing declines in revenue

- Understanding sales cycle

- Phone sales tactics and strategy

- Upselling strategy

- Weaving sales into company culture

CHAPTER 15

GO BIG OR GO HOME

A ll this work on communication, accounting, resolving our tax issues, finding a new "second store," and upgrading our sales skills took us through the middle of 2010. It was a lot, but altogether we felt good and were accomplishing some amazing things.

In May of that year, I went on a one-week cruise with my family and had a blast. As always, it was nice to have no cell phone reception and get away from work—not because I didn't like work, but because I needed to release myself from my obsessive one-track mind and get some perspective on life. During that trip, I had some time to think about what I wanted for the future, for the next year. It seemed that every other year was a growth year, so we needed a vision for growth in 2011.

A VISION FOR GROWTH

In a growing company, it is imperative that you have a vision for the future—a vision that you believe in so much, others around you cannot help but be pulled into it. The vision should make everyone's eyes get a little bit wider from a mixture of excitement, adventure, and perhaps a dash of fear. It should be lofty but achievable, with just the right amount of stretching from each stakeholder. And should that vision be realized, everyone will feel like they have personally gained through this achievement.

So I set a new goal for the business: opening four to five new stores in 2011. That's right—not one, not two, not three, but four or five new stores. I thought this goal was lofty but achievable.

When I returned from the cruise to San Diego, I called an all-managers meeting with Bryan, Richard, and Brandi. For the first time I created an agenda, so we could talk about how to make the vision of four to five new stores a reality. We acknowledged that the first store would probably be in Los Angeles County, as it was the next market north of Orange County. The rest of the meeting outlined how that was going to happen:

First, we would create an Excel analysis to help us avoid making the same location mistake we originally made in Costa Mesa. I didn't know how we would do this, but I was sure there was a way.

Second, we would create a plan for hiring and training entire store teams, so we would have them ready by the time their store opened. Again, I didn't know how this was going to be done.

Third, we needed a purchasing and installation plan to make sure all the equipment was operational when the store opened.

If we could pull this off, we would be the largest personal media transfer company of our kind. No privately owned company in the personal media transfer space had more than two retail locations. In 2011, we would either make history . . . or crash and burn.

DEVELOPING A LOCATION STRATEGY

Immediately, I set myself to the first task—creating a location strategy. The fact that I had no idea how to do this only further fueled my fire. I loved the creative process: getting my hands dirty, trying something out, deciding it wasn't the right way, learning from that, and then going to the next idea. This is where my business education had come from and where I feel the most alive. I knew, beyond a shadow of a doubt, that I could figure this out. It was only a matter of time.

During the day I would do regular work at the office, and at night I came home excited to continue my quest to crack the code that would tell us where to put future stores. I worked through the night and into the early morning nearly every day. My brain was sure that the solution was there and I just needed to uncover the path. My raw food lifestyle went out the window along with good sleep goals and daily exercise. I was back to obsession.

There was a ton of trial and error. At one point I had meetings with GIS (geographic information system) experts—which didn't lead anywhere. I then looked at demographic factors, US Census data, and lots of QuickBooks data going back to when we first became a company. I'd feel lost one moment, but then the next day find something new—a thought, a hook, a wrinkle, a small ledge to climb on and see if anything was up there. To do all this, I needed to learn new functions like VLOOKUP, and my pal Gabe was there to help me. I just kept going.

Finally, after two weeks of this—and following an exhausting eleven-hour stint at work—late one night (at 3:43 a.m. to be exact), I cracked the code. The final spreadsheet comprised tens of thousands of cells and about fifteen worksheets. Each sheet provided some necessary data to the next one. Distance tables, zip codes, wealth factors, census data, pivot tables—everything led to the finish line, the last sheet. And it told us how much we would make in each zip code in Los Angeles. Hopefully.

I trained Bryan on the spreadsheet method, and he went to work mapping out every major city in the rest of the country—yes, the entire country, not just California. By the time he was done, not only had we projected revenues for each city listed by zip code; we also had combined that data with average manager pay rates, office space rental rates, and other information to make a complete analysis on how much total profit each location could make.

Lesson Learned: Cognitive Dissonance Is the Secret Sauce of Success

I spent years tackling projects I didn't know how to do . . . yet ultimately created nearly perfect results. In the end, I gained some insight into the two elements necessary to produce these amazing results despite having no starting knowledge: *energy* (aka determination or grit) and *belief*—the belief that you are going to get to the finish line.

I believed with 100 percent conviction that I was going to accomplish the task I set out to do, and since the brain doesn't understand time so well, it was confused about the reality that I hadn't achieved that task yet. It was cognitive dissonance at its finest. When my brain thought it should be at the goal, but in reality I wasn't there yet, my brain was constantly trying to bridge the gap.

That is my secret sauce: my mind is confused that the goal has not yet been reached, so it works overtime trying to reach that goal so the world makes sense. I'm pretty sure that is why I have ideas in the middle of the night or a solution randomly pops into my head while I'm doing something else. Those ideas are coming from my brain working without me consciously aware of it—trying to bridge that gap between *where I truly am* and *where I believe I should be.*

Since we had agreed that the next store would be in LA County, we used the location analysis tool to tell us which of the county's zip codes would achieve the most revenue. The top ten projected-earnings zip codes were all around the same level of revenue, so we outlined other factors to investigate: freeway considerations, neighborhood considerations, and all kinds of other factors. In the end, Brandi pushed to find an office in Culver City.

I worked with a retail office broker to find suitable properties that were within our budget. We always took a cautious approach to leasing, preferring one-year contracts. We looked at some spots that were solely retail and other spots that were warehouses. Eventually we chose an office building that worked best for our business, because it was an ideal space for customers to visit.

Or so we hoped.

PUSHING OUR GEOGRAPHIC BOUNDARIES

Analyzing the data from cities across the nation got me thinking about our options outside of California. At around the same time, my fraternity brother Steve (the guy whose futon I slept on when I started the company) introduced me to a successful entrepreneur named Randy. We had lunch at Mister A's, a rooftop restaurant in downtown San Diego. It was my first time there. Randy said that opening an office somewhere remote and inaccessible had taught him many valuable lessons.

It made me think: if DVD Your Memories was eventually going to go nationwide, we needed to open a store in a place I couldn't just drive to when something went wrong. That would surely test our systems and show us where we needed to improve.

During our zip code search, Denver had shown itself as a good contender for our first remote location. The city calculations were average and relatively low risk, and we could fly there in a couple hours. Plus, I had a lot of family in the area. My dad had recently moved with my stepmom to Denver, and I enjoyed visiting.

Shortly thereafter, my mom attended a talk by Noah Alper and bought a signed copy of his book, *Business Mensch: Timeless Wisdom for Today's Entrepreneur*. Noah founded Noah's Bagels, grew the company to over one hundred stores, and sold it to Einstein Bagels for $100 million. After reading his book, I realized that Noah had successfully navigated a path of growing a business that shared many similarities with DVD Your Memories. He also had a unique perspective on what kind of a person becomes a successful business owner, something I had always struggled with.

As you've heard before, I'm never too proud to beg for advice. So I reached out to Noah and asked if I could get some consulting advice. To my surprise, he accepted.

Our meeting was great. Frankly, Noah was brilliant about business as well as about life in general. Up to that point, I had banked ten thousand hours at DVD Your Memories and considered myself an expert in the domain, but even without knowing much about the specifics, Noah seemed to know more about my business than I did. He had instincts beyond compare.

Noah showed such empathy about my scaling concerns, because he had been there too. And he was humble enough to share what he learned, giving me a lot of solid advice and bringing up new and interesting ideas. He also offered me a strong warning.

"You're not ready to open a store outside of California yet," he insisted.

That gave me pause. I was pleased that Noah was passionate enough about helping others that he'd take the time to meet with a complete stranger, but I didn't know how to swallow his candor.

"Your team can't handle it yet," he said. "You haven't developed the personnel resources necessary, and you'll be stretched too thin."

He wasn't against us expanding, though, and instead suggested we open more stores within driving distance. Specifically, he mentioned LA County being able to handle a few locations because it is so big.

I didn't argue with him. In fact, I told him that he was right. Opening a store in Denver was not the right thing to do. Even so, I found myself saying, "Noah, I have to take this challenge. I have to keep pushing my limits."

And with aplomb, Noah seemed to understand.

DEVELOPING OUR LEADERSHIP

With LA County and Denver chosen as our next spots, we had to start working on paying attention to the people who would be running our growing business. To start with, I had to make sure that I embraced the role of owner and boss.

Once you have multiple levels of hierarchy, those on the bottom rung look at you and treat you differently. They see you through the lens of their past experiences. Maybe they had shitty bosses in the past or overbearing parents. They bring all their perspectives and biases into their meetings with you.

Now, if you are a young company owner—sometimes the same age as your employees, like I was—you get the advantage of having no archetype for comparison. This is a gift. In my experience, those employees who have little to no experience with other bosses *really* listen to you. If you are speaking your truth and you truly want what's best for them as well, you will have an eager audience.

I took this opportunity to tell our employees what mattered the most to me. And usually it was growth—not only my own, but theirs as well. As I explained, it was their growth that would propel the company forward.

A common misconception among managers is that to hold on to their job, they need to hold their subordinates down. This is precisely the wrong thing to do. If those under you cannot move into your position, how will you ever move up? Your subordinates must be able to replace you. In fact, they should be trained to do your job better than you.

Another part of being a good boss is taking care of yourself so you can perform the job well. While I had good intentions to preserve my energy and take care of myself, I did so only in fits and starts. I'd eat raw, get sleep, and exercise for a while, and then work would consume me again and I'd slack. So I decided to do something for myself: I hired a personal assistant.

In my case, I wanted someone not only to handle random time-sucking tasks, but also to make me raw, vegan breakfasts and lunches. I hired Mark, a trained chef, who came over in the mornings for about two hours and made my meals for the day and took care of other personal tasks. It was a phenomenal decision.

Never had I indulged in something like this. Growing up, my family never even had a housecleaner, so having my own assistant felt weird. Maybe I even felt a little guilty for spending money on something I could do myself. Little by little, however, I started to change my tune.

My decision was logical, based on earning potential. The time I spent working on growing the company was more valuable to me than what I paid Mark. I have no idea what I was earning per hour back then, since I didn't track my time, but let's just say it amounted to $50 per hour. Mark made $14 per hour. If I could give up $28 to have an extra two hours a day, making me $100 more, that was a net gain of $72. I realized that hiring Mark was like hiring any employee who frees you up to work on more lucrative tasks.

Just like I had to grow personally, DVD Your Memories had to keep growing leaders if we were to grow as a company. The readiness of our future leaders was going to determine the future of the company. So I applied the same logic that led me to hire Mark to the store managers, Bryan and Richard.

Bryan was doing a lot more than just managing the San Diego store. He was constantly diverted to necessary technical projects and helping the Orange County store. It was important that one person wasn't working too hard or too many hours, because that would lead to burnout. To free him up, I needed Bryan to have an assistant manager.

Anthony had been with the company for a while and excelled as our image scanning technician. We were proud to promote Anthony to assistant manager, and he appreciated the increased responsibility and pay.

Tip: Watch for the Shift from "Me" to "Us"

Every new employee starts out in a job with the perspective of looking out "for me." This period lasts until they see enough evidence that they can trust the company, and at some companies (or for certain employees) this time lasts the entire length of their tenure. But Bryan and I learned to watch new hires and catch the moment when they went from "for me" to "for us."

You can see it in their intentions, and it is this point where their development begins. As an owner, you want to do everything you can to make sure this point arrives in the first few months. We promoted Anthony to assistant manager in San Diego as soon as we could tell that he was definitely "for us"—that he had our backs and would be extremely diligent at his job.

Richard was doing very well as the manager in Orange County, and the OC store was really taking off with the new location in Irvine. He had a unique gift among us nerdy folk—he could sell. He knew how to talk to customers and probably was the all-time best salesperson for DVD Your Memories. When the OC store was a bit behind in its sales goals, Richard would answer the phones and take the orders himself, freeing up his team to get their work done without throttling. He was also grooming a great new hire, Blake, to be the assistant manager and take some of the load off himself.

Hoping to ensure our next location would be in such capable hands as his, we began to look at bringing in new leadership.

MANAGERS FOR THE NEW STORES

With two new stores coming online soon, we needed managers for those locations. When possible, we always wanted to hire from within the company. First Richard (from the Orange County store) and then Anthony (the new assistant manager in San Diego) were asked if they wanted to move to LA and become the store manager there. Neither was interested in the position.

In late 2010, we interviewed quite a few candidates and ended up choosing Nate. He passed all the tests with flying colors. He also knew about Mac computers, which we figured would be helpful in LA as our forecasting showed us many customers there used Macs. After Nate was hired, he started training in the San Diego and Orange County stores, learning and mastering each department one by one. He ended up being a big help during the holiday season that year.

Meanwhile, Bryan and I interviewed prospective managers for the Denver store. We ended up hiring Steve, who had worked in technology and sales for most of his career and could build PCs from scratch (which gave him plenty of nerd cred). Steve joined Nate in training at our stores in California, starting to learn each department.

When both Nate and Steve had questions about vacation days, sick days, and other company policies, Brandi stepped up and created policies that met our growing needs. That was one thing I always appreciated about Brandi: whenever the company grew, she figured out what needed to be done to accommodate the growth. Whether for accounting workarounds, HR issues, or filing the correct documents for new business licenses, Brandi never had to be trained. As always, I was very grateful for this.

I had plenty to keep me busy already.

Tip: Determine How Many People You Can Manage Well

When organizing virtual teams of people who will be working from geographically dispersed locations, it is important not to be managing too many people. For me, the best number is seven: if I manage more than that, I get overwhelmed and lose track of conversations. *Harvard Business Review* mentions, in the article "Getting Virtual Teams Right," that the best virtual team size is ten people or less, and that the worst have more than thirteen members.

2010 ENDS ON A HIGH NOTE

As 2010 drew to a close, most of my days were spent with six to seven Gchat windows open, talking back and forth with Brandi, Chris, Bryan, and Richard. If I was in the San Diego office, I could also work with Bryan on something, then turn around and talk to Chris (whose desk was next to mine), and then go next door and meet with Brandi. Each of them was smart, capable, and energized, working toward our common goal. I couldn't have asked for a better team.

On December 10, 2010, the company hit $1 million in yearly sales for the first time. It was a significant occasion: we were now a million-dollar business. That is a lot of digitized slides, photos, videotapes, and film! I sent an email to notify the company of this occasion. We were truly experiencing the energy of growth. I could only hope it would carry us forward during what was sure to be a challenging 2011.

Online Resources: Advanced Business Analytics

Visit startuptosold.com for up-to-date resources on the following topics.

- Location research & strategy

- Management systems for large teams

- Sales analysis

- Growth strategy

CHAPTER 16

REPRODUCIBILITY, CONSISTENCY, AND THE FRANCHISE MENTALITY

One way to grow a business, as I mentioned earlier, is to develop a franchise mentality. We've all visited multiple franchise locations of the same company, and know the value they offer—consistency and predictability being at the top of the list. Go into any fast-food restaurant, and you know certain things will be on the menu that are the same across the country (or even worldwide), even though each store has some things that make it unique.

Simply put, there is a way that things get done, and that way is documented and trained. This all leads to predictable, measurable results, and that consistency is just as valuable behind the scenes as it is to the up-front customer experience. For the business, it means that new stores can be set up quickly: supplies, equipment, training, and layout are the same from location to location.

Although DVD Your Memories was going to have branch stores, not franchises, that franchise mentality was at the top of mind as we entered 2011. We needed easy ways to reproduce the success of our original stores, and to know which improvements we should make and which to avoid. We needed systems that were reliable and reproducible, and ways to manage them to maintain consistency. And that meant we had to train our leaders and employees in the right way.

TRAINING IS CRUCIAL

Having people perform at consistently excellent levels across a dispersed company is largely an issue of training. In the coming year, we would need to train a bunch of new people as technicians. My vision for training them included robust technical training videos that would take a brand-new hire and teach them how to do the job. These videos would show step-by-step how to run each of the four major departments in the store: film, videos, audio, and images. Editing usually didn't need much training; most of our editors had already been heavily trained and just needed to learn the editing software we preferred.

Richard had a film background, having gone to film school in Arizona and previously worked as an editor, so he took on the task of creating training videos during his free time. The first step was creating scripts for each technical training video, and each script was pages and pages long. Between creating these videos and his regular store manager duties, Richard was very busy through the end of the year.

After getting through the 2010 holidays in one piece, Richard shared the recently finished training videos. We were all blown away. The videos averaged an hour each and were well produced—not your average cell phone camera production. Now we could provide these videos to a brand-new technician, and they could effectively get their job done after one viewing.

With that feat accomplished, Richard had earned himself a

promotion to a newly created corporate position: director of training. And it couldn't have come soon enough.

We were already busy placing ads for new employees to join the upcoming LA County store. For Denver, the plan was to hire two technicians to help Steve at the start. Normally, we would have only one technician ready when we opened a store, but since Denver was so far away, we had to err on the side of caution. There were also the expected technician turnovers that came once or twice a year in the San Diego and Orange County stores.

With Richard starting a new position, we needed to agree on what the central goal would be, and then pull every tool, trick, and technique together to make that central aim a reality. The director of training's goal was simple: to have the best-trained media transfer technicians in the world.

With that lofty goal agreed upon, it was time to meet and create a plan for Richard's new position. Going into that meeting, neither Richard nor I had any formal background in training.

"How are we going to make this plan?" Richard asked.

"I don't know," I replied, "but I am one hundred percent sure that given two hours and two Red Bulls each, we can figure it out." By the end of that day, we had outlined the plan that would allow Richard to train the best techs in our industry.

The essence of our training plan was to create a curriculum, just like a school would. Our curriculum included modules to train every aspect of the job, from order taking to order processing to finalizing and double-checking. At the end, the technician would take a final exam proctored by Richard. Each module would be tracked via Google Sheets so that the store manager or any of the corporate team could track the new technician's progress.

We retained our previous strategy for new technicians: make them earn it. Before successfully passing their final exam, new hires were considered "technicians in training." This meant they were not issued a lab coat and could not answer phones or take orders by themselves. But once they had completed all modules, including the final exam, they would "graduate" and be accepted into the ranks of their store.

The final exam sometimes took more than eight hours to complete. Richard had built in some tough technical problems that technicians in training would have to diagnose in order to finish. In one part of the videotape final exam, Richard tricked them by replacing an audio cable with one that looked the same but didn't work. This gave some of the techs problems, but we needed to simulate every situation in which they would find themselves.

Although we didn't have spies infiltrating other media transfer companies, we couldn't imagine any other company went to such great lengths to make sure their techs were prepared for anything. I was extremely proud of Richard's achievement. The techs were proud of themselves, too. And when it came to doing the work, we were making fewer mistakes than ever before.

ESTABLISHING AN OFFICIAL STORE OPENER EXECUTIVE

While Richard was developing our training videos, I asked Bryan if he would like to move up from store manager into a new corporate position in early 2011: store opener. He would not be working for an individual store any longer; instead he would be working for the good of the entire company. Bryan accepted the position, and we outlined the plan for the transition, which would start later that year.

Making the store-opening process as simple as possible was part of our franchise mentality. We knew that in future years, it would take more than just Bryan to open new stores. To practice what we preached about training others to do your job better than you do it yourself, we started out with the intention of being able to easily train other people to open stores. That way Bryan could keep moving up and the company could keep growing.

As you can probably predict by now, we didn't know how to develop the position of store opener, as neither Bryan nor I had done it before. But as with everything we didn't know how to do, we just jumped right in. More than ever, we were constantly doing things that we didn't know how to do. My new mantra became *Two hours and two Red Bulls, and we'll figure it out!*

Figure 18: A surprise gift from the LA County store—before it even opened!

Bryan and I worked together, starting with the vision and goal for the position. We wanted the company to have a document, or even a thumb drive, with all the instructions for opening a new store. The final result outlined everything from choosing an office broker and a location to deciding which equipment to purchase (and from where) and even how many copies of office keys to make. The document included pages and pages of digital documents— living documents that Bryan constantly updated and followed, tested and refined. And we were going to need it all.

MORE EMPLOYEES, MORE IMPROVEMENT IDEAS

As we began to hire and train more staff, I was starting to get more suggestions on ways to improve our systems. This was ultimately a good thing because incremental improvement was one of the hallmarks of our company. I was still meeting with each new employee on their first day to tell them how much we value suggestions.

I had to decide whether it was a good use of my time to investigate these improvement ideas. We were in total offense mode now. And by "offense," I mean doing the things necessary to propel the company forward, creating our own tasks that would grow the business—the opposite of being in defense mode, where you are fixing mistakes, answering emails, and simply reacting to what tasks other people are giving you. Diving into a system that was already working was not something I wanted to be doing, but I needed to maintain the integrity of the company and what we stood for. Everyone's voice had to be valued and heard.

So I came up with a few steps to handle the situation when employees made a suggestion:

1. Thank the employee for making the suggestion.

2. Determine whether the suggestion would help or would be a step backward.

3. Decide whether the value of that suggested improvement was worth the hassle of changing in order to implement it.

4. Have the person who made the suggestion work on creating the new system.

The third and fourth steps happened only if I determined that the idea would in fact improve the company. At DVD Your Memories, our systems were revered. By this time we had a lot of tacit knowledge, and our systems had evolved to make sure random problems that had crept up in the past would not happen again. Many times, these were problems that the current technicians had never encountered. So it was a big deal if someone could improve a system.

Furthermore, the fourth step might sound like a way of discouraging the suggested change. But in truth, it gave the person good experience in working with their manager, Bryan, or me on the project. And in the end, if the project was tested and worked, we not only implemented it across all stores but named the new system after the technician who developed it. For example, Elliot, an audiophile who worked in the San Diego store during this time, was young and talented—kind of like a younger version of Bryan. Elliot had many suggestions for improving the videotape department's workflow, and we came to use a number of them throughout the company.

ADJUSTING TO THE LARGER SCALE

By this time, Richard, Bryan, Brandi, and Chris were all on the corporate team. Richard still worked out of the Orange County store and had his own office for training. Bryan, Chris, Brandi, and I were based in San Diego.

I was busier than ever, working with Bryan on creating a store opening plan, working with Richard on the training plan, and now acting as general manager of two (soon to be more) stores. This happened every time we grew. And I realized that I needed to adapt because the workload was a bit stressful. I loved every minute of it, but the hours were becoming long, and the amount of data I needed to process and act on every day was immense.

The first thing I did was switch from daily store sales reports to weekly totals. The best rule for data is that you should receive it only if you will act on it—and there was no way I could act on one bad day of sales for any store. There just wasn't enough time. Weekly sales totals were good enough. Plus, whenever I learned about a good day of sales, I would feel overjoyed, and when the day was crap, I felt damaged. So psychologically, too, this was healthier, as it would curtail the highs and lows of my mood.

I also needed to reduce the data points for individual stores. There were so many KPIs at this point that it overwhelmed me and, I'm sure, the store managers as well. We needed to simplify—to focus on what was important. I thought about this a lot. The more I thought about it, the more I came back to three measures of success I'd previously identified:

1. The customers need to be happy.

2. The employees need to be happy.

3. We need to make money.

As a manager, I felt great—like everything was under control—if all three of these measures were met. If any of them were not met, I knew what I needed to work on. The store managers, too, needed to know what was important. They knew that if they were making money, their customers were happy, and their employees were happy, then when I came to visit their store, I would be happy with their performance. And they knew that if one of the conditions was not satisfied, then we were going to work on that.

I wanted managers to feel like they had control of their store and my trust that they could achieve that control. If they handled everything successfully, they would enjoy my visit. This type of management was important for each store, because it gave the managers self-motivation and ownership of their own destiny.

Lesson Learned: Hiring Is an Adventure

As we prepared to open the LA and Denver stores, hiring was a top priority. I learned that it was also an adventure.

During one interview, I was asked out on a date; that was a first. But another interview that I'll never forget was Robert's. He came in and totally failed his computer skills test. Then at 6:21 p.m. that same day, I received an email from Robert, thanking us for interviewing him; attached was a ten-page, single-spaced Word document that outlined the questions he missed—and the correct answers.

I have no idea how he remembered the questions, but we were so impressed that he took the time to learn and follow up, we hired him. Robert ended up being one of our best technicians.

PAY BECOMES AN ISSUE

Part of the trifecta of my general manager agenda was to ensure the employees were happy. For this, I was still using the survey we had developed several years earlier. Most of the feedback—90 percent—was positive. Employees were excited about the company and the prospects for themselves. However, a few employees had complaints about their compensation.

As I read those particular reviews, I felt terrible. I had spent many hours making the company an enjoyable place to work. Bryan was instrumental in bringing up the technicians' viewpoints about new systems and policies, and making sure that their voices were heard. We had incentives for good performance. We funded quarterly parties. We offered a health insurance program. And we had just instituted a profit-sharing plan that included not only managers but every single technician as well. The negative feedback hurt, and I became defensive.

I talked to Bryan and Brandi about this feedback and tried to reason a way out of it. Our conclusion was that if the technicians didn't like the pay, then they shouldn't have applied for the job. If they didn't know what the job would be like, then they should find a better-paying job now that they realized the amount of work they'd be doing for the pay. This is a free market, I figured, and this is what needs to happen. If we started losing technicians or couldn't hire great people, then we would soon learn that we had to pay more. But our technicians stayed, and we didn't have any problems finding and hiring additional qualified technicians.

Months later, I still felt bad about the employee feedback. My gut was telling me something was wrong. The nagging feeling was the same one that arose in the past when Brandi mentioned instituting a health insurance plan. Except this time, I chose not to listen.

LA IS OPEN FOR BUSINESS

On February 7, 2011, we opened our new office in LA. Bryan had done a lot of work to pull this off in just a few months. Everyone was excited to see how the new store would do. We had tested the market there a few months prior using Google AdWords. Basically, we made it look like we already had a local store and counted how many clicks and phone calls we received. The test showed this store had huge potential.

The LA store was an instant hit, doing five times the business that the Orange County store did when it was first opened. We needed to hire employees fast.

Steve, the soon-to-be Denver manager, was still training in the San Diego and OC stores when we got wind that his twenty-eighth wedding anniversary was coming up. We decided to surprise him with a ticket home and time off so he could be with his wife on that special day.

Everything was looking positive. But if you've run a business yourself, you know that even at the best of times, your luck can turn around quickly—as I was about to find out.

Online Resources: Corporate Team Strategy

Visit startuptosold.com for up-to-date resources on the following topics.

- Corporate training

- On-boarding corporate team

CHAPTER 17

RUNNING A COMPANY CAN SUCK

B y spring 2011, the Denver staff was hired. After their train-ing in California was done, we sent them back to Denver and worked hard to get the store open. We were utilizing our best practices from all we had learned from our first three stores. Overall, I was confident that my new corporate team could handle anything, and as it turned out, that belief would be put to the test in many different ways.

In fact, we were about to confront so many headaches, I have to list them by number.

HEADACHE #1: CONSTRUCTION

Our lessons learned from the first three stores led us to spend more money on equipment and build-out in Denver than we had ever spent before. "Build-out" is where a new tenant (us) would get some changes made to the physical location. Using Microsoft Visio, Bryan diligently created the optimal build-out plan for each department based on the projected revenue of the Denver store.

He had already diagrammed everything, down to each chair and Ethernet outlet, and found that we needed to pay about $25,000 in build-out construction expenses.

We learned right away that construction equals a giant headache. The approvals, the red tape with the city, and the snail's pace responses meant we were losing thousands of dollars a day, without any movement toward the necessary build-out. We couldn't leave the Denver employees out to dry, with no office to work in, so we paid them full time to work from home. We tried coming up with things for them to do, but realistically, it was busywork—nothing that would generate money for the new location. We severely underestimated the time it would take to get the office move-in ready. It was hard to keep Noah's warning out of my mind: "You're not ready to open a store outside of California yet."

HEADACHE #2: A FAMILY CRISIS LEADS TO INTROSPECTION

In the midst of the challenges with getting the Denver store location revamped, I got some very troubling news from my dad. He had just been diagnosed with stage 4 cancer.

My dad is a techie. He is the one from whom I got my love of technology, the one who taught me to recognize computer components and build computers. Growing up in his house, I lived with a PBX telephone system, a phone, and a computer in each room, and learned how to use all types of computer programs, from spreadsheets to accounting software to programming a calculator with BASIC. We also shared a name; I was the fourth in a line of Chuck (Charles) Temples. I wanted to be close to him during this difficult time.

My dad was thinking about what would happen if he died, and he would talk about those types of plans. I asked him what he would do if the chemotherapy sessions worked and he beat the cancer. I was looking for him to say that he would go out and travel the world, and do the things he had always wanted to do.

This also made me think about what I wanted to do before I die. I knew that I wanted to travel, but more important, I wanted to work on the bigger problems of the world. Preserving memories is a fantastic thing to do, but I always thought I could do more. And I figured that with all the experience of growing my business, I was now better prepared to work on bigger problems.

Watching a parent struggle, as all their hair falls out and they are unable to think straight, does things to your soul. It made me think a little differently, a little more deeply.

Not only had I begun to think about my mortality and what I wanted to do moving forward, but the nagging pangs of the employee feedback about compensation resurfaced. The truth was, I was making enough money to give my employees more *and* grow the business. But instead of taking care of the employees by increasing their pay, which would have made everyone feel good, I decided that the stress I felt was normal and the employee complaints were normal. I convinced myself that I had nothing much else to learn—that my growth curve had flattened.

As funny as it may sound, I didn't even contemplate increasing pay to get over this hurdle—and I contemplated everything twenty-four hours a day. Like I mentioned before, any part of your personality that needs work will show up in your business magnified. In this case, my personal frugality turned into greed. I was addicted to keeping money. If you have grown up with a mindset of scarcity, then you may feel compelled to hold onto your earnings, as I did. I don't have a solution to this powerful problem because I never solved it myself.

I was probably offended. I was probably hurt. I was probably rationalizing why the free market system said I didn't need to pay anyone more money. But in truth, I had more than enough and simply was unwilling to give more to others. Looking back, there are only a few things I regret, and this is one of them.

I had started DVD Your Memories to find my limits. And some of the furthest limits were the ones I could barely notice, let alone face at this time. This was my limit, and I couldn't even see it.

And we were about to be hit by more bad news . . . then more bad news . . . and even more bad news.

HEADACHE #3, ROUND 1: THE BOOKS ARE BEING COOKED!

On top of the Denver issues and my family crisis, I discovered that Barbara, one of our newer employees, was cooking the books in an effort to outperform everyone else. Ambition is a good thing until it's not.

Without going too much into detail, she was overestimating the original orders from customers. That led us to believe that several stores were doing more business than they were. It affected our hiring strategy and caused us to pay more money in taxes that were calculated based on estimated sales. But most important, it was dishonest.

No one in the company had ever done something like that before. It is a tough decision to fire anyone, but firing Barbara was the right thing to do. Being dishonest was something you cannot allow to continue inside an organization, or it will infect others and spread like a cancer.

HEADACHE #4: STOLEN CASH

In the fashion of a corroding cancer, a couple days later, Brandi told me that after her last count, more than $4,000 was missing from our cash box in San Diego. This was another first. Each store had an open cash box, and we had never locked it during the day. To me, that was one of the things I was most proud of—having a company from which no one stole.

I was devastated. After having to fire someone for being dishonest, now we had to deal with someone else being dishonest. I spoke with a couple of friends who owned businesses, and they couldn't believe I didn't lock up my cash boxes or at least have a camera monitoring them. I had been sure that if you showed someone trust, they would prove that trust to you. Maybe I was mistaken.

Anthony, the newly promoted assistant manager in San Diego, set up a hidden camera by the cash box and waited to see what it would find.

HEADACHE #5: LOSING OUR ORGANIC SEARCHES

After hearing about the cash box news that morning, we discovered that very afternoon that our internet traffic on the website had dropped sharply. We investigated and discovered that all our organic search was gone!

Even though paid search was very lucrative for us, organic search—the search listing, in Google and other search engines, that you don't have to pay for—accounted for a large chunk of our sales. Chris had worked every day for the past year to increase our organic rankings. We were ranked in the top three organically for most of our profitable keywords. Losing our organic ranking would severely impact our ability to make money.

Even worse, we didn't know why it had happened.

HEADACHE #3, ROUND 2

If I thought that week couldn't get any worse, I was wrong. I soon discovered that Barbara—the employee we had let go for bad bookkeeping—was defaming us on social media and threatening to sue us. By the end of the week, I had more crises on my hands than ever before.

HEADACHE #4, ROUND 2 (ANYONE GOT AN ASPIRIN?)

So many feelings were swirling around in me, I couldn't keep track of them all. I didn't have a great coping mechanism, and my brain was working overtime trying to figure out these various challenges. Mostly, I was just spinning in circles.

I was so stressed out from these crises that I reluctantly canceled birthday dinner plans with the woman I was dating at the time. There was just no way I could relax and enjoy my time with her when my brain felt like it was at war. She didn't take my flaking on her too well and decided to end our relationship until I had more time for her. I couldn't really blame her.

While in my office over the weekend, I noticed the janitor in the building. We said hi to each other, and I didn't think anything more of it. When Monday came around, Brandi said that another $180 had been stolen over the weekend. We checked the tapes, and sure enough, at some point there was a shadowy figure fidgeting with the filing cabinet we used to lock up the cash box. The cash box was seen taken out of the room and a few minutes later put back into the filing cabinet. We couldn't quite make out the face of the culprit. Then it dawned on me that I had seen the janitor come in around the same time.

I checked the time I had been in the other office: it was within ten minutes of the theft on the recording. We contacted the janitorial company and made a police report. The janitorial company said our janitor admitted to stealing, but only the $180.

After many calls with the local branch of the janitorial company as well as our landlord, the janitorial company told us that they wouldn't reimburse us for the entire theft. The landlord had been good to us for a very long time, and we didn't want to ruin that relationship even though the landlord had hired the janitorial company. We also didn't want to have a big legal fight on our hands over this $4,000.

We looked up more information on the janitorial company, however, and learned they were part of a national chain. This meant they had a corporate headquarters.

Tip: Always Work with Headquarters

Whenever a local business you are dealing with is part of a national chain, it is always more effective to go to someone in the head-quarters. I knew this from having just four stores. If a customer was upset and wanted to talk to me, I embraced such conflict resolu-tion as part of my job description. But I still despised doing it.

It was important to keep our customers happy, but dealing with a conflict could really mess up my day. Usually, if the value a cus-tomer was asking for was a few hundred dollars or less, I would give them what they wanted. It just wasn't worth the time of cor-porate staff to get more involved. And this is how it is for every national company I've dealt with.

We told the local manager that we would be forced to create a small claims court lawsuit if the company did not reimburse us for what their employee had stolen. In fact, most likely that large janitorial company had an insurance policy for exactly this type of event, so the company would not be out any money. The other advantage to threatening a small claims lawsuit was that it would force the company to come to San Diego in order to fight it. Having someone from their corporate team come all the way from out of state would cost hundreds if not thousands of dollars in travel expenses—all to fight a case in which they were at fault and we had the proof on camera.

Needless to say, the company cut us a check for our losses.

HEADACHE #6: MISSING CUSTOMER FILES

One morning Bryan was contacted about some abnormalities with the scanning computer systems. Specifically, some large customer orders were gone.

"Gone?" Bryan asked. "Just wiped clean?"

The answer: "Yup."

Bryan went to check this out, and he not only confirmed that the files had been deleted, but also discovered an entry in the store's router indicating that a remote user had logged in the night before.

Richard joined Bryan from Orange County and started running logs on when files had been deleted as well as using recovery programs. We also called up a good friend of ours who owned an IT company. He inspected everything and found out that after being unceremoniously terminated for accounting fraud, Barbara had remotely logged in to the Mac mini computer in the office. That computer was linked to every other computer on the network. The time of the remote access entry matched up perfectly with the log of when the files on the computers had been deleted.

We were all furious. I felt attacked. And it wasn't just me. It was the company, the technicians . . . They were scared and stressed out, and frankly so was I. We never thought that someone would do something so corrupt. Thousands of dollars of finished or in-progress customer orders had been lost.

It is a terrible feeling to know that someone is trying to hurt you.

But when there is an attack, the amazing thing is, people band together.

The staff would never be able to rescan all the media that had been deleted in time for the holidays that year. They would be underwater for months, and when Nate, the LA store manager, sent in his resignation, we had to start looking for a new manager. Richard, Bryan, and I knew we needed to get the LA store some serious help.

Our only option was to work nights while the rest of the staff worked days. We found a studio apartment near the University of Southern California and rented it monthly. Bryan and Richard didn't hesitate for one second about living at the apartment and working the night shift until things were under control. Those guys really saved the day. They provided certainty and consistency at a time when everything was in utter chaos.

Now that's teamwork.

HEADACHE #3, ROUNDS 3 AND 4

There we were, driving up and down Southern California, living in a cramped studio and working nights to get LA back on track, when Barbara wrote us a letter. Not only had she mismanaged our books and then bad-mouthed us on social media, but now she had decided to sue.

Barbara brought up a few different reasons for threatening us with a lawsuit, but only one piece made sense: she thought she should have gotten paid for overtime during the first few months she worked out of the office.

Barbara didn't want money. All she wanted was for us to change the conditions of her termination to "no cause," meaning that her termination wasn't due to anything she had done wrong. This change would have implications for her receiving unemployment as well as for us paying unemployment insurance.

I was so pissed, I wanted to give Barbara a giant box of nothing. The problem was, as my attorney advised, the costs of going to court could run toward $10,000. If we changed the status to "no cause," on the other hand, it would cost us nearly nothing. Changing Barbara's termination would pretty much have no effect financially, whereas fighting her would have a big effect.

After some discussions, I reluctantly gave Barbara what she wanted. I don't know whether fighting would have sent a strong message or not fighting made us seem weak. In the end, it came down to what was most advantageous for the company. Financially, by fighting the case, I would have spent thousands of dollars— money that would not just have come out of my pocket, but would have impacted profit sharing for the whole company.

And yet Barbara was still not done with us.

Suddenly, multiple suspicious accounts started posting negative Yelp reviews about our company. These accounts had been recently created, and we had no record of such people ever placing an order. This was a big deal because of how much effort we put into our customer service—and because we know many customers came to us because of our high Yelp ratings.

At around that time, thanks in large part to the LA store, we became one of the highest-rated media transfer companies in the entire United States. Only one other company—a slightly bigger company in New York that had been around longer—had more positive reviews than we had. If we had a bad review, we would do everything we could to make things right. Now we were being attacked on that front, too.

Chris ended up spending quite a bit of time working with Yelp to get the false reviews taken down. One of the reviews seemed to come from a legitimate account, which meant that Yelp couldn't take it down. But the culprit was no match for Bryan's internet prowess. Bryan was able to perform a reverse image search on the Yelp account in question: the profile image matched with one of Barbara's friends on Facebook. That was enough proof of collusion for Yelp to remove the bad review.

HEADACHE #7: REACHING 90 DEGREES

We were in the middle of a marathon with a long way to go. Bryan, Richard, and I were taking turns living in LA County and working nights. I was still flying to Denver regularly, as the store there was brand new and had some issues with turnover. The OC and San Diego stores were doing fine, but I really had no time to think about them.

Adding insult to injury, one more headache arose at around the same time when the air-conditioning in the LA store stopped working. Los Angeles can get very hot, and we had at least fifty computers running in that office along with tons of monitors. But it was still surprising when the room temperature got to 90 degrees. Unfortunately, the building management was not very responsive the first couple times we contacted them.

When I was just starting out in business, I didn't want to hurt anyone's feelings. Now, I had no time to think about feelings. When something wasn't up to our standards—and working in 90-degree heat was far beyond our standards—my temper flared up quick. It is easy to get something fixed when you threaten to withhold your rent.

I was about to discover my temper.

I DISCOVER MY TEMPER . . . AND THE SILVER LININGS

It really was one problem after the next, and I had no patience left. My diet was all messed up because I was never home, always traveling between stores. Mark, my personal assistant, had left to study culinary arts in France, so I was back to trying to manage my personal life. My sleep wasn't good because of all the stress. I realized that most of my personal relationships were screwed up because I worked too much and always put the business first. During the height of the crises in LA and Denver, I had spent only two nights at home in San Diego.

I was starting to lose it.

I would start drinking beer, and not even the good kind, just to get myself numb enough to make the drive back up to LA for the millionth time. One time when Bryan and I were working late into the night in LA, I broke down on the floor and cried. Things were just too out of control, and I couldn't see any way to escape this prison.

With all these headaches piling on one after another, I had to find a way to focus on the silver linings. The cash box theft had been taken care of, and we could still be proud to say that no *employee* had ever stolen from the company. The Denver store had finally opened, and we were not losing as much money every month. As for that problem with our organic search disappearing, we figured out that a WordPress plugin had affected it. We disabled the plugin, and the organic search returned.

What's more, as far as we knew, no other privately owned personal media transfer company had four regional stores. That accomplishment felt really good. We had worked our tails off, and now we could be proud that we had done something no one in the history of our industry had done. Despite what might happen in the future, no one could take that away from us.

In the middle of all these events, Brandi wrote me a note on her three-year anniversary, telling me how much she appreciated being part of the team. It was such a nice moment in the middle of all this chaos.

It was good to discover all these silver linings within my personal rain cloud.

The way the whole company had rallied together throughout this difficult time made me so proud. I felt like they each had my back and had the company's best interests at heart. Without the commitment of my team, I'm sure the company would have unraveled at the seams. I was savvy enough to realize that I had the best, most dedicated team a person could ever hope for.

CHAPTER 18

RECUPERATION AND FORGING AHEAD

We did not meet the goal I had set at the end of 2010: to open four or five new stores in 2011. But with everything we went through that year, I was still proud of all we had accomplished—including opening a store in a location outside of California.

On the home front, quite a few qualified candidates came in for interviews for the LA store manager position. After the Barbara debacle, we were much more careful in looking for red flags. One fellow came just a few minutes late to his interview, and I turned him right around. He was befuddled. I told him that first impressions are a big deal, that actions during interviews are magnified, and we couldn't have a manager who arrived late.

"Good luck with your job search," I said. In my experience, 100 percent of the people who have come late to their interview have been habitually late as employees. I knew I wouldn't regret holding my ground.

Lesson Learned: If It Looks Like a Duck . . .

People are who they are. If someone is late for an interview, they will be late coming in to work. If someone is unprepared for their interview, they are likely to lack preparation at other times—or they just don't care.

I used to give everyone the benefit of the doubt, always believing the best, always believing that the situation influenced what we saw during an interview. But after hiring so many employees and then seeing how their employment worked out, I can safely say that 100 percent of the time, what you see is what you get. Don't expect people to change.

We wound up hiring from within. An audio-video tech in the LA store named Brian had shown himself to be a super-quick study as well as creative with technology. I mistyped his name in my Google contacts as "Brain," which was apropos. I kept it that way, and he's still Brain to me.

With Brian in charge of the LA store, we were starting to catch up again after the debacle with the deleted files. It was good timing because the holiday season was upon us. My job now was to make sure the company was running as smoothly as possible so 2012 could be a prosperous year—and to enjoy that smooth running.

"VIRTUAL CHUCK" MANAGES BY THE NUMBERS

I had enough time to do a little bit of sales training, which helped a lot during the season. With four stores to manage, I quickly became overwhelmed with the number of tasks I had to manage. But it wasn't just my own tasks; each of the new managers also had many weekly tasks that needed to get done. As the general manager of the company, it was my job to make sure that the managers did their jobs.

A lot of stigmatization surrounds the idea of micromanaging—when you watch or help someone under your supervision so they complete the tasks they are responsible for. Micromanaging can put a lot of pressure on employees and cause all kinds of problems. Usually bosses who micromanage do so because they don't properly know how to train and are nervous that their employees will screw something up.

On the other hand, proper management has a system in which employees are held accountable for their responsibilities. The boss's job is to create a system that manages their employees. Having to constantly manage an employee is a sign that something in the system is broken.

To avoid micromanaging, I created a new system called "Virtual Chuck"—a spreadsheet that would be used to manage each store. Within the spreadsheet, each responsibility was listed across the top columns. Each row had a date range that corresponded with the week. If a task recurred weekly, then the cell was left blank, and the manager would fill it in with the date it had been completed. If something happened once a month, I would shade and mark the cell with an *X* for the weeks when they didn't need to complete the task. That way, the managers could look at their individual store worksheet and know what needed to get done that week.

Within the same document, I made a master worksheet that had the name of each manager across the top (columns) and the week down the side (rows). For each month, I left one blank row to input the customer service scores for each store.

Each cell referenced the count of items that were missing from the corresponding week. Then I used conditional formatting to color-code the number of items missing. For example, if someone had everything done, then that cell turned green. If they had a few items missing, it was orange. And if they had four or more items missing, it would be red.

Similarly, for the customer service scores (according to the scale we had set in 2008), a 4.6 or above would show green; 4.5 to 4.59 would show orange; and anything less than 4.5 would show red. With this system, I could look at just one screen and see whether each store was on track.

Additionally, if we added or reduced the items a manager was responsible for, I could train them and then, with just a few clicks, change the system so that they had a built-in reminder.

If a store was getting its items done, they would be fine. I would still visit them on a regular basis, but these would be fun visits. If a store was not getting stuff done, then I would spend my time there figuring out why.

I thought all this tracking might be annoying for the store managers, but to my surprise it was quite the contrary. I received lots of positive feedback when implementing this system. The managers liked having something they could base their week on, something impartial that helped remind them what needed to get done and when. And it gave them control, because they knew what would happen if they completed everything and what would happen if they didn't.

ONE LAST 2011 HEADACHE

There we were, right before Christmas 2011, feeling good that we had gotten through the most challenging year ever. And then, four days before Christmas, I got the worst Christmas present of all time: I was served with a lawsuit.

WEEK ENDING	STORE MANAGER 1	STORE MANAGER 2	STORE MANAGER 3	STORE MANAGER 4	INTERNET MARKETING	STORE OPENER
12/9/2011	0	0	1	0	3	0
12/16/2011	0	0	0	0	3	0
November Customer Service	4.8	4.7	4.73	4.61		
12/23/2011	0	0	2	0	3	0
12/30/2011	0	0	0	0	9	0
1/6/2012	0	0	1	0	3	0
1/13/2012	0	0	0	0	3	1
December Customer Service	4.61	4.68	4.73	4.74		
1/20/2012	1	0	2	0	3	0
1/27/2012	0	0	1	0	3	0
2/3/2012	0	0	0	0	3	0
2/10/2012	1	0	2	0	3	0
January Customer Service	4.73	4.72	4.72	4.75		
2/17/2012	0	0	2	0	3	0
2/24/2012	0	0	2	0	3	0
3/2/2012	0	0	5	0	3	0

Figure 19: Visual management.

This time it wasn't Barbara; it was from a competitor in Orange County. I examined the lawsuit, and two things stood out. One, the checkbox designated that this was a claim for over $25,000. And two, the general claim was that our company had written a bad Yelp review about their company, and this lawsuit was for those damages.

The bad review had been posted from—you guessed it!—Barbara's Yelp account. Apparently, this company had been trying to contact Barbara about the negative review for months. After Barbara was terminated, she wrote back to the OC competitor saying that I (yes, me personally) must have gone on her computer or hacked her account and written that review.

One thing was certain: I was motivated to get that competitor off my tail.

As we did some research and looked closely at the company's website, I was taken aback at the blatant rip-off of our own website. No other company website in our industry used the term "tape-smart pricing," so when I saw our custom graphic with our phrase "tape-smart pricing" copied *exactly* on the competitor's website, I called our attorney.

Within about a week, the competitor asked us to drop our charges of copyright infringement, and in exchange they would drop theirs. It was tempting to go through with the legal route now that we definitely had the upper hand. But the goal was never to get embroiled in legal matters; the goal was to run a business. Plus, I still had two new stores with new managers to worry about.

We dropped the case and never heard from the company again.

ENJOYING THE FRUITS OF MY LABOR

After a rough 2011, I spent 2012 taking it as easy as I could. The trend was clear: growth year, rest year, growth year, rest year. Now I was in a rest year, so I took the opportunity to take vacations every chance I got. I knew when I was motivated, and I knew when I was not. Now was the time to make sure I got the rest I needed to get motivated again.

The first part of 2012 brought some light amid the mania. Our upgraded website was done, complete with store chooser functionality. Now our one website functioned as five websites. This allowed us to target SEO better, since the city names were on each city-branded site. Theoretically, it also gave us lower bids with our paid search efforts, because matching the search term with words on the website was encouraged by Google.

Karina, a friend from college who had gone on that first spring-break trip to Thailand, had a little extra time in the mornings, so she decided to take over the role of my personal assistant. Besides making raw food in the morning, she would also make sure I went down to the apartment gym and got a workout in. Now, with proper diet and exercise, I could think a little better.

During this time I also started a new personal experiment. With four stores open and making money, and for the first time not needing to save for anything, I found that my income became substantial. I had always needed to be frugal, buying clothes at Target or the thrift store, making sure I didn't go out to eat at the most expensive places, and so on. Now, I wanted to see what it was like to have money and spend it on things I'd never been able to afford before.

I went shopping with Karina at Nordstrom's instead of Target. We bought some pants and a couple shirts. The shirts were $100 each! Those were the most expensive shirts I've ever bought, and I still have them. When I needed sheets for my bed, instead of going to Target to get forty-dollar sheets, I splurged on Calvin Klein sheets.

Those are the big things, but it was really the little things that made more of a difference. At the start of my journey, I was stealing food from my roommates. After building one successful store, I didn't have to choose the least expensive option on the menu. And now, with four stores, I didn't even look at the price tag or the bill at the end of a meal. I would even order a drink or two and not worry about it. This was amazing!

SURVIVING THE HARD TIMES

Sometimes you look back at things that happened and say, "This was one of the hardest times in my life." If you are a first-time business owner, you will be confronted with those times while you learn. Each time you grow, there will be growing pains. What makes you successful or not will be your grit. Do you give up easily when things get tough, or do you persevere?

Something happens on a personal level when you go through a lot of hard times and come out on the other end. I can't remember a time in my life when I had it easy; there was always a challenge of some sort. But over the past year I had faced crisis after crisis, and somehow had gotten through the worst of it.

There are two ways to survive through a crisis. One way is to end up broken, in pieces, with some mental roadblocks where you had to psychologically escape to survive. I have experienced this in the past. And then there is another way, when you realize that you are bigger than those problems because they didn't stop you. Your brain has adapted to handle the stress of those crises.

Mental stress is a subjective experience. You have control over it. You may not realize it until you get through it the first time and then face it again, but you learn, you adapt, and eventually you realize that these crises are what make you into the person you are.

Nassim Taleb's book *Antifragile: Things That Gain from Disorder* describes how systems that are "antifragile" get better as a result of being under stress. Maybe not in the moment, but in the end, getting through hard times while holding onto your values is what gives you character. And that's how it worked out for me. Those threats of 2011 fundamentally changed who I was.

A benefit of this change in my character was evident when it came to women. All my life, I had to work so hard to get a date. Now, suddenly *I* was being asked out. It was the weirdest and most amazing thing. I had a new outlook on life: I could get through anything. *I am smart and capable, and I will outwork anyone to find a solution* was my new mindset. That gave me confidence, and women somehow picked up on that.

Now that I had my diet, exercise, and relationships under control, my overall health and happiness improved by leaps and bounds. And when I was happy, other things in life clicked.

BUILDING ON OUR SUCCESS

Around the middle of 2012, the LA store started to take off again. It was now our largest store by revenue, even at only about one year old. I started digging into the data and found out that a high percentage of customers had used Yelp as their referral source.

Then I looked at the number of 4- and 5-star reviews in aggregate, by month, on Yelp.

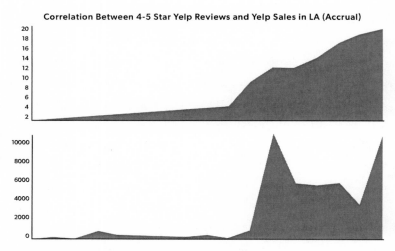

Figure 20: Timing of Yelp review and sales in the LA store.

Yelp had quickly become a top referral source, and the cause of this seemed to be the fact that we were quickly rising to the top of the heap in terms of customer ratings on the platform. I also learned that Robert, the technician in LA whom we almost didn't hire, had created an email template that he was sending to customers, which was causing them to leave those Yelp reviews. That email was quickly shared with the rest of the company.

Finally, I found that the length of time between a customer picking up their order and our standard practice of calling to thank them correlated to the propensity of positive Yelp reviews. In other words, the quicker we thanked the customer for doing business with us, the more likely they were to leave a positive review.

After seeing the great effect Yelp had in LA, we decided to work on getting all stores up to this same level of customer approval. I made a spreadsheet for each of our stores and tabulated how many reviews they had, broken down by stars. This allowed us to know how many more 4- or 5-star reviews we needed to bring a store's average up to at least 4 stars.

As the adage goes, "What you measure improves," and so did our Yelp reviews. Little by little, customers were giving us more and more positive Yelp reviews. We were also proactively following up with the few negative reviews we received. By the end of 2012, I couldn't find another media transfer company on Yelp that had as many 4- and 5-star reviews as we had.

I could honestly say that we were quickly becoming the highest-rated media transfer company in the world.

KEEPING CULTURE ALIVE

As a company grows, the culture usually weakens. Conversations, corporate teams, and the random funny jokes—all things that foster a strong culture—start to become diluted. Although we had instilled culture into the company a couple years earlier, we could see a need to revisit the issue now that we were twice the size.

One thing that proved unexpectedly useful was my commitment to meet with each new employee on their first day. I always reviewed our training module, "Intro to the Company," with them and explained the history and growth of DVD Your Memories. The bigger the company got, the harder it was to schedule this meeting. But on the flip side, as we grew bigger, taking the time to meet meant a lot more to each new employee as well.

By hearing the story of the company, new employees could learn about our values and culture: how we were built on a foundation of hard work, grit, doing the right thing, being the leaders in technology, keeping a lean organization, frugality, and so forth. It also showed that we valued them, that it was worth it to have the company owner spend half a day with a new employee right when they started. Finally, it was a good reminder to me about where we had come from, and why I'd invested my life into the company in the first place.

While having consistent values and ethics was important, we found it natural for each of our stores to create their own personality within our common culture. The OC store was really into movies, acting, directing, and all that. The LA store was eclectic and more into music and art. Not surprising, the Denver store was more outdoorsy. The San Diego store was diverse; they were into photography, filmmaking, making music, and video games. But we needed something to connect us.

I ended up finding a web software platform called Yammer, which acted as a sort of Facebook but for companies. You could send messages to the company wall, and everyone would see it. Or you could private-message individuals. And of course, you could comment by text or by symbol, similar to Facebook with the Like button. These days, Slack would be my recommended software to foster culture within a team or company.

Culture is subjective and intrinsically hard to measure. On Yammer, however, technicians and managers were posting funny pictures, tons of memes, videos of craziness at work. It was entertaining. Most remarkable were the personal projects that some employees shared. And of course, we posted the important company announcements. If the fun was good-natured, anything went!

It was also important to foster the spirit of continual learning. For example, we announced a $100 bonus for anyone who took an online course that related to our business or their specific job. We could not stand by on our laurels, because business moves fast. And now that we were the market leader in every new county we entered, someone would be coming for us.

DYNAMIC EQUILIBRIUM

Although 2012 was a non-expansion year—no new stores added—we didn't just sit around counting our blessings. Just like in previous years, we looked for new ways to increase sales using our current staff.

We ended up creating a video production company and a business division. They were both fun ideas and a blast to work on. But we always remembered the principle established in *The 22 Immutable Laws of Branding*: The scope of your services is inversely proportional to the strength of your brand. Both of those offshoot businesses had their own websites and phone numbers. They were associated with DVD Your Memories, but not part of the company itself. For bookkeeping, they had their own column in the P&L, so I could track all expenses and revenues separately.

Now that we had four stores, we were hiring new technicians all the time. Richard was doing a great job training them. The operational systems we had created were working well. But as I tried to rebuild from the toll that 2011 took, I began to think about where I should direct my energy next.

And that's when I met Sean.

Online Resources:
Managing Multi-Location Businesses

Visit startuptosold.com for up-to-date resources on the following topics.

- Keeping culture alive

- Upgrading reporting systems

CHAPTER 19

THE BIG DECISION

I met Sean, a former vice president of a worldwide, billion-dollar retail electronics company, in early 2012 when he came to see me in San Diego. He was not just vice president of sales or marketing or operations—he was the vice president of North and South America for the company. When he said that he had been scouting companies to buy and grow, and that DVD Your Memories interested him, I couldn't help but bite at the bait.

We met up for a beer. Sean told me that after looking at more than fifty companies, he realized that most of them were run very poorly, or the numbers didn't add up to what the business owner said. So he was here to make me a proposition.

He and I connected right away over RTS computer games, where all players can make moves at the same time, and we have been friends ever since. Sean has the same theory as I do about how RTS games relate to business—a theory that, to date, I've never heard from anyone else. That connection led to an offer that had me rethinking my involvement in DVD Your Memories.

GAMING AND BUSINESS DECISIONS

I believe RTS games to be one of the most thoughtful types of electronic games ever developed. (The other is turn-based strategy, where players can only move if it is their turn.) Most RTS games go like this:

You start out with a small number of units. Some units are for attacking, some for defending, and some for gathering resources. There are different types of attacking and defending units, and they all have different strengths and weaknesses compared to one another—think of rock, paper, scissors. And the resource-gathering units allow you to build up your base and more units.

The basic strategy for an RTS game is to protect your resource-gathering units while attacking your opponent and disrupting their production. Use the new resources to grow your base and expand into other territories, doing the same thing there. Eventually you might have multiple bases and command hundreds of different units.

Growing up, I spent countless hours playing these games—starting with Command & Conquer (both the original and Red Alert) and StarCraft, then moving on to Total Annihilation, and eventually to the game I still play now: Supreme Commander. There were many others in between, but those were the ones I put the most hours into. And the way I was building DVD Your Memories was like how an RTS game works: Start with nearly nothing. Build up the first base while learning the game. Each employee had their strengths and weaknesses, as did I, and we were constantly figuring out how to use our strengths against the market to take market share.

Now, remember that in RTS games, you have hundreds of units that you give orders to. You must remember what they are supposed to be doing, and then check in on them so they don't get ambushed or go off course. Commands are given via a series of waypoints or patrol areas. This is also like business in that you set objectives and then check in at regular intervals to get updates.

Micromanaging is like watching one of your units move and constantly clicking to give them direction. Managing, on the other hand, is telling them what their target is, making sure they have all the tools to reach that target, and checking in if you hear they need help. (In an RTS game, there is always an audio signal that a battle has started somewhere.) At the top, it is the job of the commander (CEO) to remember all the different battle groups, where they are going, what resources are needed, and whether you have enough resource gatherers getting the right resource—not to mention ensuring that you are protecting those resources and eventually finding holes in the enemy's defenses.

I was taken aback when Sean talked to me about RTS in terms of business expansion . . . but not as shocked as when he expressed his official interest in buying DVD Your Memories.

SELLING OR QUITTING?

Wow! Initially, this was very exciting—to have someone of Sean's caliber interested in the company and telling me how well we were doing compared with other, larger firms. This was like getting a perfect report card after six years in the school of hard knocks. As good as I felt about finally knowing for certain that I had created something special, however, I also felt an immense anxiety about selling.

It *was* selling, wasn't it? Then why did it feel the same as *quitting*?

Now, don't get me wrong: 2011 was the toughest year of my life—opening two stores, the Barbara firing and subsequent attacks on the company, working endless nights, never being home, fighting a lawsuit, obsessing over a couple of negative employee reviews, and the cash box debacle. I'll admit there were times when the stress got the best of me, and I contemplated giving up. But I didn't quit, and my team didn't quit. We all made it through together.

Was selling the company equivalent to quitting on my team?

As an entrepreneur, I knew that selling a business for a profit is the definition of success. In fact, some might argue it's the entire point! I came to terms with this fact, yet I still felt a responsibility for the employees of the company, especially those who had been there the longest. They had sacrificed to grow this business. I had a guilty feeling because they had never quit on me—and now I would be essentially quitting on them.

It took me awhile to realize that I needed to give Sean more credit. He had grown a company from zero to $350 million and had successfully managed hundreds of employees. Our company was about 1 percent of that size. Sean's experience was light-years ahead of mine.

Furthermore, after spending time getting to know him, I was certain that Sean was not a jerk, as so many high-level businesspeople can be. He was a genuinely nice and caring person. Sean was more qualified to take the company to the next level than I was.

The experiences I had at DVD Your Memories had taught me so much. While I loved the company with all my heart, I am undeniably an entrepreneur. I love growth and new challenges. I aspired to use the skills that the company taught me for bigger, more important projects in the future. I also understood the focus it took to be successful, and I needed to be fully in or fully out—for me, there was no middle ground.

Then there was the all-important issue of freedom. DVD Your Memories was fueled by the freedom I felt the night of my graduation, looking up at the boundless sky, contemplating how far I could go with no rules to follow or authority figure to answer to. The journey had taken me from broke college student to financially independent adult. I had become a business owner with twenty-seven full-time employees and more income than I knew how to spend.

But by the middle of 2012, it was clear that the very thing that had freed me felt like my captor. I decided it was time. I was going to sell the company.

SEAN MAKES AN OFFER

Around September 2012, Sean sent his letter of intent to purchase DVD Your Memories. I made a couple of small counters to his offer. The final agreement was a sale price in the seven figures. This was the first time I had ever thought seriously about being a millionaire. It didn't seem real.

I almost felt guilty for agreeing to that much money. In the months that followed, I wavered back and forth, sometimes thinking that I got the better deal, sometimes thinking that Sean got the better deal. Eventually I realized that the price paid must have been fair, because I couldn't figure out which one of us fared best.

I had already been working with Sean, sharing with him every detail of the business. But now that we had a formal letter of intent, the due diligence process was underway. "Due diligence" refers to all the legal documents and flood of paperwork that must be completed in order to sell the assets of a company. It is a coordination of lawyers, escrow companies, state regulation boards, bankers, and company owners. Sean and his lawyer worked with Brandi to figure it all out.

There was one sticking point to all of this. I had planned to have a company retreat in Temecula, California, the first weekend of November 2012. Corporate members would come the first night, and then store managers would come the following morning. Sean thought it best if we announced the sale of the company during that retreat, since all the management and most of the technicians from four stores in two states would be together that weekend. I agreed with him. However, the business brokers strongly advised against it—and for good reason.

If the sale was not completed by November, and I broke the news of the impending sale and the sale did not go through—it could be disastrous. The other risk was that Sean would see something at the corporate retreat that he didn't like, get cold feet, and call it off.

There were many reasons not to have Sean present at the retreat, and I spoke with him about my concerns. Sean assured me that nothing could happen at this retreat that would deter the sale, and I had worked with him enough to trust him. So I agreed to have him come out to Temecula and announce the sale before the deal was final.

It was risky, but I felt it would be so much worse to have everyone come out for a company retreat and not tell them. Everyone in the company deserved to be together as they learned about the transition. I was more nervous about something else: making the announcement.

Everyone who was part of the company deserved to hear the truth about why I was selling. I owed them that and a lot more. But speeches, especially super-important ones, still made me obsessively nervous. The next few months were spent making sure the company would be set up for when I left—and practicing my speech.

WELL, THIS IS AWKWARD

November arrived. The sale of the company was moving along, but it would be another six weeks at least before all the sale documents were completed. The decision had been made to announce the sale during the retreat weekend. I still had no idea how to break the news.

For months, I had felt like a liar because I had to keep this important secret from almost everyone. I also felt like a sellout, because I was taking the money and leaving the company to someone I had only known for a few months. At least the cat would be out of the bag soon, I reasoned, and then I could stop hiding.

Our corporate team was meeting at the retreat on Friday, and by Thursday night I still hadn't written up a formal announcement. But I knew this moment was too important to leave it up to an impromptu speech. I started writing late Thursday night, and the peaking emotions kept me up through the night. As I was writing this speech, there were moments that left me in tears. It was the ending of everything I had worked toward for seven years—and the most important thing in my life.

On Friday, Bryan and I collected supplies for the weekend, including the most important things: two Xboxes and eight controllers, so we could play four-on-four Halo tournaments. We started eating and drinking and having a good time while the rest of the corporate team arrived.

Richard was working on making a new "Intro to the Company" video for training new technicians and wanted to interview me to tell the story. Man, what an awkward situation—trying to make a video about the company right before I was about to tell him I was leaving.

As the sun was setting, Brandi, Bryan, Keith, Richard, and I assembled on the high bar outside for my announcement. I had the speech in my hand. Then I looked up at them and thought about how much each one of them had given to this company and how much I enjoyed working with them. My head went back down to my speech, and I lost it.

I spent the next few minutes crying as quietly as I could with my forehead pressed down against my speech while everyone waited silently. Eventually, blurry-eyed, I got through it and delivered the speech. We spent some time talking about what it all meant and how we would all move forward.

The next day, the store managers and some technicians arrived. I gave them a similar speech, and it was much easier this time. Sean waited so we could have an hour or so to digest the news before he arrived. After some questions and reassurances, Sean came—and he fit right in. He made a short but effective and humble speech, telling us about how impressed he was with our company and the dedication of everyone he had met.

We spent the rest of the day playing billiards and Halo, and just enjoying ourselves. And before I knew it, the corporate retreat was over.

MOMENT OF TRUTH

Sean really liked our team, and our team liked Sean. It was a relief to finally shed the burden of secrecy. It was looking like November would be my last month as owner of DVD Your Memories.

Then, on November 13, Sean alerted me to an alarming sales trend. Instead of being our typical best month of the year, our sales were trending toward being the worst month of the entire year. I looked at the numbers, and he was right. Sean was scared. I was scared. We had to figure this out.

We looked over all the stats, and nothing stood out as being irregular. There was a dip in our blog traffic, but that couldn't have accounted for the massive drop in sales, since we didn't get a lot of business from just blog traffic. Internet marketing clicks were steady; time on-site was steady; phone calls were steady. So why no customers?

Either the industry had changed since the company had heard

the news about the impending sale, or everyone who worked there had gotten spooked.

The very next day, I called a companywide meeting via video chat. I had no idea how it would go. For the first time, I had no transactional leverage with my own company because I was no longer its owner. In fact, I was calling a meeting that, technically, I didn't have the authority to call.

Had the team's perceptions about me changed? In their mind was I now simply the guy who'd sold out? Would my words sink in, have meaning, and elicit a proactive response, or would they go in one ear and out the other? Had I lost the strong connections that I had worked tirelessly to achieve? Suddenly, this meeting felt like it was the most important meeting of my entire life.

I told the corporate staff and managers the situation with the sales numbers. Then I told them how this looked to the guy who was about to buy the company.

"This is serious," I said.

I didn't plead with them. Instead I pushed away the insecurity that ran through my mind and decided to trust all that we had built together—to believe firmly that the culture and camaraderie we prided ourselves on was not just bullshit. I called upon their passion to do things that had never been done before, a passion I knew every team member possessed.

Memories—of our like-mindedness, our togetherness at company retreats, and our ingenuity when blindsided by backstabbers or thieves—anchored me as I asked the managers to help me one last time. I needed their help in figuring out how to get out of the bind we were now in—with the closing date impending.

All the roads lead to right here, right now. Whether I had really achieved success with this company would be revealed, and it would leave an indelible mark on my life. Was I the leader I had set out to be, or not? This was the moment of truth.

I'm not sure what happened, or how the managers relayed the information to their staff, but the very next day was a monster. And we had more monster days to come. Sales started pouring in. Customers who had been deliberating massive orders suddenly decided to place them. It was weird. The last three days I owned DVD Your Memories were the three biggest days in our history. We ended up blowing away our all-time sales record.

THE DEAL IS DONE

The last day of November, the wire came in from the escrow company. The money was in the bank, and that was it. For the first time in almost seven years, I was no longer the owner of DVD Your Memories.

My responsibility for the livelihood of twenty-seven employees was over.

The constant stress over gaining new customers was gone.

The incessant worrying about each store and how each employee was doing in their job was no more.

The omnipresent concern that one day we would lose a customer's videotape was gone.

And I felt a freedom that I hadn't felt in a long time.

My contract stipulated that I was to work for four months to help with the transition of the company to new ownership. It had been seven years since I had worked for someone else. Engaging in tasks that someone else asked me to do was so much easier than constantly trying to figure out what to do. I could just do my best, with all the risk being on someone else's mind. I felt a hundred pounds lighter! I gave as much input as I could, but ultimately the responsibility for all decisions rested with Sean.

December was busy, but all the stores made it through in one piece. The company was strong. It had survived the transition of ownership, and no one seemed upset with me for selling the business. And as the end of the year rolled around into 2013, it felt great to see the company thrive in someone else's capable hands.

MY LAST DAY

I was out in Denver on my final day of work, on March 29, 2013. My dad, with the support of family, great doctors, and especially my stepmom, had beaten his cancer into remission, and things were looking up. His illness and fear of death had made me ponder my own life and goals—and as I was about to close one chapter of life and start the next, luckily my father was able to do the same.

The Denver store was about to close that day when a customer walked in. I looked around at the technicians, and everyone was busy. I hadn't taken more than a handful of orders in the past year or so, but what the heck . . .

As I walked over to greet the man, I thought, *This is the last customer I'll ever help here. As of tomorrow, I'm retired from this business.*

And then it all hit me—how much this company had helped me grow as a person. I started the company right after college, just a kid with one client. I had no idea about management, about responsibility, about the mindset it takes to be successful. I had given DVD Your Memories everything I had, and in return it gave me everything, too.

I greeted the customer, and we sat down to look over his order—just one videotape he wanted to convert to DVD. I took his information and filled out the order form, the same yellow triplicate form that Bryan, Brandi, and I had written and rewritten over and over again . . . the one Richard and I revised when he started his new training position . . . the one we ran out of during the first holiday season we were in business.

I asked the customer his name.

He said his name was Chuck.

Online Resources: Exit Strategy

Visit startuptosold.com for up-to-date resources on the following topics.

- How to estimate your company valuation

- Making sure you have the contract right

- Negotiating strategy

- How to set up a company for a sale

CHAPTER 20

AFTERMATH

Can you guess what I did immediately after selling DVD Your Memories? Remember my advice to celebrate whenever you can! I rented a big house and threw a three-day party where more than fifty friends showed up to celebrate. I bet you can guess what I did after that, too: yes, travel. I went on a three-month, fourteen-country trip connecting with old friends and meeting many new ones.

These celebrations not only solidified a job well done, but also provided an end to the greatest challenge of my life.

THE FIVE ELEMENTS OF STARTUP SUCCESS

It has been ten years since I sold DVD Your Memories, and since then I've gotten an MBA, broken 80 in golf a number of times, and won a prestigious business competition. I also failed at a startup; became COO of another startup (a juice business) that then became a million-dollar company; and then became a top influencer for the personal electric scooter market, eventually selling that business.

Over that time, I've gained a lot of insight into what it takes to be successful at a startup business. Here are the five elements in a nutshell:

1. **Seek the right product–market fit.** This is mandatory because if people don't want or need what you are selling, the business will never flourish.

2. **Believe you will succeed.** Convince yourself that you will be successful, that it is just a matter of time. Since the brain doesn't understand time, it will work doubly hard to make your success a reality. And when you have this belief, the next two elements come pretty easy.

3. **Work with grit and determination.** Keep working at something, and don't give up the first time it gets difficult. In fact, the more difficult something is to start, the harder it will be for others to compete with you.

4. **Pursue positive energy.** Try to enjoy the struggle and savor the experience you are going through, as it might be something that happens only once in your lifetime. Certainly it will be something you can tell stories about when you're older! Being positive helps the brain make mental connections that are simply not possible with negative energy, and new connections are how you'll progress in business.

5. **Be unafraid to learn.** No one who engages in a startup knows what they are doing. If you are too proud to do what it takes to learn, then you will certainly fail—perhaps slowly and painfully. Ask questions. Ask for help. Read books when you encounter situations you aren't familiar with. And remember to fill in your knowledge gaps—you don't have to be great at everything, but you must be competent.

"SO, IS IT WORTH IT?"

I was asked this difficult question more than any other while growing DVD Your Memories. During the first few years, I would probably have said no. But by the end, when the business was more stable and financially secure, I changed that answer to yes.

Going from startup to sold was a process of growing up, from naive college graduate to savvy business owner. I learned about and experienced hard work, struggle, dedication, responsibility, management, and what it takes to succeed. Maybe I would have learned these lessons somewhere else, but surely not at the speed mandated when you're a business owner.

Selling the business and getting a big check is a short-term reward; more important is what that money does for you. I still need to work, but now I can choose to work only on the projects I'm passionate about. This is the real blessing.

I became who I am through DVD Your Memories; the business was my teacher. Now, my passion is to be a guide, a mentor, a counselor, or whatever you want to call it for others going through their own journey of entrepreneurship. I connect to those who, like me, are not interested in the path of mediocrity—those who are trying to create something great, something that has never been done before. Because really, the only reason to invest so much in something is to make it the best it can possibly be.

ACKNOWLEDGMENTS

F irst and foremost, I want to thank the corporate team, store managers, assistant managers, and every technician at DVD Your Memories from the phase of ideation through the sale of the company in 2012. Without your hard work and dedication, the company would never have been successful and this book would have never been written.

I want to give a special thanks to Bryan, Brandi, Richard, and Chris for believing in the vision of the business and making that vision a reality.

There are many people who did not make it into the final version of *Startup to Sold* but were instrumental to the success of the business: Marques Fields, John Hermes, Ben Alpert, Dan Weiss, Mike Seib, and Thi Buhlmann.

I want to thank my family living in Ventura from 2006–2012. They welcomed me with open arms and empty washing machines, listened to my business problems, and provided a much-needed respite during the toughest of times.

I want to thank my late friend Karina Gershler for being there for me, whether as an employee for a day, my personal assistant, or a good friend to talk to.

Special thanks go to Jackie of JF Computer Solutions for all the computer help during those years, especially during the tough times.

I want to thank Tim Bennett for being my go-to for internet marketing expert advice and for consulting on this book.

Another big thank you to Will Tams of the Creative Spark agency for creating the wonderful cover of this book, consulting on book names, and being a great pickleball partner.

To Seth Gilmore and Marily Benson (my mom), thank you for reading and giving feedback on early editions of this book, titling advice, and cover designs.

I also really appreciate all my wonderful editors, Sue and Amy with Greenleaf Book Group, but also to Michelle Matrisciani for believing in this story and encouraging me to find a publisher.

I also want to thank my stepmom, Claudia Temple, who introduced me to mindfulness. I could write another entire book on how mindfulness was a major key to my success in business (and in life).

ABOUT THE AUTHOR

 **CHUCK TEMPLE** is a highly successful entrepreneur that has founded three million-dollar industry-leading companies. Started on a shoestring and with no additional funding, the first of these companies, DVD Your Memories, became one of the largest and most successful personal media transfer companies in the US.

By the time DVD Your Memories was acquired in 2012, the multimillion-dollar company had twenty-seven full-time employees with four offices in two different states.

Having begun his entrepreneurial path with no formal business education, Chuck received his MBA from UC Davis with a focus on entrepreneurship in 2016, the same year he won first place in the prestigious Big Bang! Business Competition.

Chuck, along with his business competition partner, founded the Electric Scooter Guide in 2019, which became the world's leading resource for the personal electric scooter market within a year. While Chuck successfully exited the Electric Scooter Guide in 2022, he continues to be recognized on the street as an influencer due to the hundreds of YouTube videos and live shows he and the Electric Scooter Guide team created.

Chuck currently resides in the San Francisco Bay Area with his wife and young son. He currently teaches go-to-market strategy for UC Berkeley Extension and consults for small- to mid-sized companies. When not teaching or consulting, you can find him at the local parks playing with his son or running a pickleball club.